Pursuing Diversity:
Recruiting College Minority Students

by Barbara Astone and Elsa Nuñez-Wormack

. *ASHE-ERIC Higher Education Report 7, 1990*

Prepared by

Clearinghouse on Higher Education
The George Washington University

In cooperation with

Association for the Study
of Higher Education

Published by

School of Education and Human
The George Washington University

Jonathan D. Fife, Series Editor

Cite as

Astone, Barbara, and Elsa Nuñez-Wormack. 1990. *Pursuing Diversity: Recruiting College Minority Students.* ASHE-ERIC Higher Education Report No. 7. Washington, D.C.: The George Washington University, School of Education and Human Development.

Library of Congress Catalog Card Number 91-60268
ISSN 0884-0040
ISBN 1-878380-04-4

Managing Editor: Bryan Hollister
Manuscript Editor: Barbara Fishel/Editech
Cover design by Michael David Brown, Rockville, Maryland

The ERIC Clearinghouse on Higher Education invites individuals to submit proposals for writing monographs for the *ASHE-ERIC Higher Education Report* series. Proposals must include:
1. A detailed manuscript proposal of not more than five pages.
2. A chapter-by-chapter outline.
3. A 75-word summary to be used by several review committees for the initial screening and rating of each proposal.
4. A vita and a writing sample.

ERIC **Clearinghouse on Higher Education**
School of Education and Human Development
The George Washington University
One Dupont Circle, Suite 630
Washington, DC 20036-1183

This publication was prepared partially with funding from the Office of Educational Research and Improvement, U.S. Department of Education, under contract no. ED RI-88-062014. The opinions expressed in this report do not necessarily reflect the positions or policies of OERI or the Department.

Why Is the Recruitment of Minority Students An Important National Concern?

Present and future trends in population growth and in participation in higher education reveal that people of color in the United States are a dramatically increasing but seriously undereducated segment of society. By 2000, minorities will account for roughly 30 percent of the population (U.S. Bureau of the Census 1990c). Even now, 27 percent of all public school students in the 24 largest city school systems are minorities (Hodgkinson 1986). Yet for nearly all minority groups, high school graduation rates are significantly lower than for the majority, and entry rates of college-age minorities into higher education are actually shrinking. For example, almost half of all 18- and 19-year-old Hispanics and one in three African-Americans that age have not completed high school. The proportion of 18- and 19-year-olds from these groups enrolling in college, despite big increases in that population, are lower now than before. In fact, the gap between minority and majority students entering college was wider in 1988 than it was in 1976 (American Council on Education 1989).

With greater and greater numbers of minority youth coming of age, the problem is no longer one purely of social justice. Government and industry alike have noted the potential economic effect of these alarming trends in education (American Council on Education 1990). With the projected increases in the minority population, the situation threatens to affect the national economy: Given the present level of minority education, the potential shortage of qualified workers equipped to meet the needs of the market is a serious concern (*Economist* 1990b; Hodgkinson 1983). Institutions of higher education are being called upon to exercise leadership in helping to address these problems before they take on even more critical proportions. The recruitment of minority students must therefore not only focus on more aggressive strategies to recruit those students who are already well prepared but also encompass long-term initiatives to improve existing educational conditions.

What Is the Institution's Role in Pursuing Diversity through Recruitment?

Higher education institutions are the traditional centers for scholarly debate, research, innovation, and change in social matters. Increasing the presence of minorities and of minority perspectives in all aspects of the college and university is, in its broadest sense, a question of social change. Universities can provide vision, energy, leadership, and direction to other institutions, from school systems to government to business and industry, first to establish firmly the goal of excellence in minority education and then to pursue and achieve it (American Council on Education 1988). Through investigation into the subject of minority education and the effectiveness of responses at various levels, higher education institutions can bring the issue into focus. But beyond the social role, colleges and universities need to determine the ways in which diversity will be incorporated locally by identifying what the problems are with regard to their own institution. Are minority enrollments and graduation rates low and, if so, why? Do minority students feel welcome and are they part of the college community? Colleges need to evaluate their mission, institutional objectives and policies, and the allocation of resources with minority education in mind. An initiative to recruit minority students will affect, and be affected by, institutional concerns from curriculum to campus life. To be effective and make a real difference, therefore, the goal of increasing the presence of minorities on campus should be conceived as an institutional priority and an institution-wide goal.

How Are Minority Students Distinct—From Each Other and from the Majority?

Because they share many common concerns, people of color are frequently referred to as a single group. In fact, however, this population of African-Americans, Hispanics, Asian-Americans, and American Indians consists of an enormous variety of people from different racial, ethnic, language, and cultural backgrounds. As a group, clear distinctions—social, economic, and educational—can be made between minorities and the majority. A much greater proportion of almost all minority communities have lower income, higher unemployment, and poorer education, both in terms of quantity and quality (Richardson 1988; U.S. Bureau of the Census 1990c). Additionally, the obstacles they encounter include some that are not part of the experience of most majority students, even those who are disadvantaged. Limited proficiency in English and racial and ethnic prejudice are two examples.

With regard to higher education, however, the nature of the problems in each minority community is somewhat different, and each situation calls for solutions that are informed and responsive to the needs of each community. Preparation for college, language proficiency, immigrant or nonimmigrant (or refugee) status, time in the United States, gender, cultural influences, and financial condition are only some of the factors that vary from group to group and could have more or less significance in a particular minority group's educational profile. Further, important distinctions exist within minority groups. For example, low rates of graduation from high school are a serious problem in all Hispanic communities and significantly affect the number of Hispanic students who enter college. In the Puerto Rican community, however, school dropout begins in junior high school, reaching levels estimated to be as high as 80 percent in some school districts (Fernandez 1989). Consequently, it is considered the single most alarming educational concern in the Puerto Rican community. Recognizing and understanding the differences within and among the various minority populations are essential elements in a successful strategy for recruitment, and they are an important preface to the larger goal of achieving cultural diversity in higher education.

How Is the Recruitment of Minority Students Related to Other Institutional Concerns?

Because the ultimate goal in recruiting minority students must be graduation, recruitment is not an objective that can be pursued in isolation. The better integrated it is with the college's educational programs and services, the more opportunity it will have for success. Admissions and financial aid policies, strategies for retention, and opportunities for transfer are some of the areas intricately tied to recruitment that therefore can share common objectives (Carnegie Foundation 1989; Lenning, Beal, and Sauer 1980). Organizing strategies for recruitment that combine the human and financial resources of all these areas can be cost-effective. Above all, however, it will disseminate minority recruitment throughout the institution.

Effective recruitment of minority students should not only be coordinated with many different areas of the institution but also enlist the participation of people from different departments and at various levels of responsibility to work in concert as part of a comprehensive plan. Nontraditional models of recruitment teams can have significant success. Administrators, faculty, and staff from academic departments, including ethnic studies programs and centers, student services, and special program offices, such as economic opportunity programs, can be organized to participate in the institution's strategy for recruitment.

Who Should Recruit, When, Where, and How?

Even when a formal structure for recruiting minority students exists, the function is commonly located in one of several different areas within a college's organizational structure. The recruitment of minorities can be administered through the regular operations of the admissions office, by a specially appointed officer, or through a variety of other possibilities. Rather than the location of the office, however, it is the institution's commitment to improving the education of minorities that will ultimately endow recruitment with its potential to be effective (Christoffel 1986). In this sense, the leadership and involvement of top administrators are fundamental.

Ideally an institutionwide effort conceived as a process rather than a program, recruitment of minority students would optimally engage all constituencies of the college—faculty, administrators, staff, and students—in a well-developed and deliberate plan designed to achieve specific, reasonable goals. The plan should be based on a comprehensive institutional audit reflecting the profile and present educational situation of minorities at the institution. It should be cooperatively designed, including the perspectives of those who will implement it, and should delineate the methods and resources designed to achieve its objectives within a stated time. Finally, it should be monitored, evaluated, and periodically modified to reflect changing conditions and to capitalize on aspects that emerge as being particularly successful.

ADVISORY BOARD

Alberto Calbrera
Arizona State University

Carol Everly Floyd
Board of Regents of the Regency Universities System
State of Illinois

L. Jackson Newell
University of Utah

Barbara Taylor
Association of Governing Boards of Universities and Colleges

J. Fredericks Volkwein
State University of New York–Albany

Bobby Wright
Pennsylvania State University

CONSULTING EDITORS

Brenda M. Albright
State of Tennessee Higher Education Commission

Walter R. Allen
University of California

Louis W. Bender
Florida State University

William E. Becker
Indiana University

Rita Bornstein
University of Miami

Paul T. Brinkman
National Center for Higher Education Management Systems

Robert F. Carbone
University of Maryland

David W. Chapman
State University of New York–Albany

Jay L. Chronister
University of Virginia

Linda Clement
University of Maryland

Mary E. Dilworth
ERIC Clearinghouse on Teacher Education

Mildred Garcia
Montclair State College

Edward R. Hines
Illinois State University

Don Hossler
Indiana University

William Ihlanfeldt
Northwestern University

Joseph V. Julian
Syracuse University

Jeanne M. Likens
Ohio State University

Dierdre A. Ling
University of Massachusetts

Sherry Magill
Washington College

Jerry W. Miller
American College Testing

James R. Mingle
State Higher Education Executive Officers

Richard W. Moore
California State University–Northridge

Bernard Murchland
Ohio Wesleyan University

C. Gail Norris
Utah System of Education, State Board of Regents

Edward H. O'Neil
Duke University

Robert L. Payton
Indiana University

Joseph F. Phelan
University of New Hampshire

Laura I. Rendón
North Carolina State University

Steven K. Schultz
Westmont College

Robert L. Sigmon
Wake Medical Center

Charles U. Smith
Florida Agricultural and Mechanical University

Sharon P. Smith
Princeton University

REVIEW PANEL

Charles Adams
University of Massachusetts–Amherst

Richard Alfred
University of Michigan

Philip G. Altbach
State University of New York at Buffalo

Louis C. Attinasi, Jr.
University of Houston

Ann E. Austin
Vanderbilt University

Robert J. Barak
Iowa State Board of Regents

Alan Bayer
Virginia Polytechnic Institute and State University

John P. Bean
Indiana University

Louis W. Bender
Florida State University

Carol Bland
University of Minnesota

Deane G. Bornheimer
New York University

John A. Centra
Syracuse University

Arthur W. Chickering
George Mason University

Jay L. Chronister
University of Virginia

Mary Jo Clark
San Juan Community College

Shirley M. Clark
Oregon State System of Higher Education

Darrel A. Clowes
Virginia Polytechnic Institute and State University

CONTENTS

FOREWORD

Over the past few years, the *ASHE-ERIC Higher Education Report* series has published several reports dealing with the issues of diversity, including:

Affirmative Rhetoric, Negative Action: African-American and Hispanic Faculty at Predominantly White Institutions, Valora Washington and William Harvey. Report No. 2, 1989.

The Challenge of Diversity: Involvement or Alienation in the Academy?, Daryl G. Smith. Report No. 5, 1989.

"High-Risk" Students in Higher Education: Future Trends, Dionne J. Jones and Betty Collier Watson. Report No. 3, 1990.

From these reports, several general conclusions are easily drawn:

• The concern over diversity is increasing.
• The issue of diversity not only concerns the strength of our society's social fabric, but also is becoming increasingly central to our economic well-being.
• Higher education institutions can and should play a major role in educating a diverse citizenry that will produce leaders capable of developing solutions for the issues of diversity in our society.

Much of the literature on minority students develops conclusions based on aggregate data. These publications clarify the general need by comparing the number of minorities graduating from college with the population as a whole, revealing that a major problem exists.

While that assessment is accurate, it is not very useful. A more fruitful examination would study the process from beginning to end and identify each important step along the way. A process similar to quality management, this method helps correct problems long before a failure occurs.

Following this logic one step farther, ensuring graduation of adequate numbers of minorities requires effective recruitment, appropriate academic advising, constant nurturing, and attention to both the academic and nonacademic student life throughout the process. In other words, for recruitment to be successful, an institutionwide value must be present, constantly reinforced by leadership at all levels, that develops an atmosphere conducive to the graduation of minorities.

In this report, Barbara K. Astone, director of retention programs, and Elsa Nuñez-Wormack, associate dean of faculty and associate professor of English, both of The College of Staten Island, City University of New York, review the available current research and literature on the recruitment of minorities. They examine demographics, the institutional structure, and topics on recruitment, offer general recommendations for institutions, make suggestions for further research, and discuss the basic elements and implementation of a recruitment plan.

The recruitment and retention of minorities is an issue that higher education will continue to face throughout the decade. This situation will not go away, for the percentage of college-bound minorities will continue to increase for the foreseeable future. As an institutionwide problem, it requires institution-wide attention, leadership, and solutions. Academic leaders must get all faculty involved in the process. Institutions must provide sufficient student support services. The entire college community must become intellectually as well as morally sensitive to the importance of ensuring the diversity of the institution.

Jonathan D. Fife
Series Editor
Professor and Director
ERIC Clearinghouse on Higher Education

INTRODUCTION

*Minority students in increasingly smaller numbers arrive
at colleges and universities from backgrounds as diverse
as those represented by white students. They come from
Republican, Democratic, Independent, apathetic, poor, rich,
and middle-class homes. They are dropped off at airports,
train [depots,] and bus stations, or emerge at college gates
from station wagons, convertibles, and coupes driven by
single parents, two parents, no parents, uncles and aunts,
grandparents, themselves, and strangers. Some arrive in
taxis. They come from homes where English is spoken impec-
cably, where it is spoken [with an accent], where it is bro-
ken, where it is not spoken at all.*

*Often they have been recruited as vigorously as first-
round draft choices . . .; sometimes they find themselves at
the gates of the only college they ever wanted to attend[, but]
frequently they arrive at colleges whose names and locations
were unfamiliar to them only weeks before freshman orientation. . . . In spite of their diversity, they are lumped into
a group identity called "minority student"* (Pemberton
1988, p. 9).

After more than 20 years, the percentage of minorities graduating from institutions of higher education, relative to their
representation in society in general, has actually decreased.
This result can be attributed to several factors. A major study
published by the Commission on the Higher Education of
Minorities reports that, compared to whites, significant
numbers of minorities are lost at each juncture along the
"educational pipeline" (Astin et al. 1982). First, minorities
drop out of high school at a debilitating rate. Recent studies
have found the Hispanic dropout rate to be well over 60 percent in some cities and, among Puerto Ricans, closer to 70
percent (Fernandez 1989). Second, significantly fewer students who graduate from high school enter institutions of
higher education; those who do for the most part do not
directly enter senior colleges. Third, most minority students
in two-year colleges do not complete that degree, and among
those who do, many fewer go on to receive a baccalaureate
degree. Finally, minorities in four-year colleges who either
transfer from two-year schools or enter directly leave before
graduation at a rate that is two to three times greater than for
whites (Astin et al. 1982). In the meantime, the urgency of

graduating minority students in significant numbers has taken on a completely new dimension.

The 1980s signaled increasingly important changes in demography. While the overall U.S. population growth rate is as low as it has ever been, about one-half that of the late 1950s, minorities account for a steadily increasing percentage of the population, reflecting the comparable youthfulness of these groups to nonminorities and growth rates two to 14 times greater (Estrada 1988). Immigration is a primary factor in minority growth rates, and presently 6 million of the 14 million immigrants in the United States are of school age (Hodgkinson 1985). Together with the higher number of births occurring in minority populations, it means that an ever-greater proportion of secondary and postsecondary students will be minorities.

As we enter the 1990s, the social, economic, and educational condition of most racial and ethnic minorities in the United States continues to lag behind that of the majority white population: Unemployment is higher, income is lower, and years of education are fewer. The poverty rate for racial and ethnic minorities in the United States is two to four times greater than that for Americans in general, according to 1980 and 1986 figures. In education, severe disparities persist for almost all minority groups, compared to nonminorities.

Today, the goals of access and academic success for minority students are no longer matters of concern only, or even principally, to the minority community. The demographic and economic realities becoming increasingly evident to government, industry, and the media are studied and reported so frequently now that issues involving minority education have moved into the national arena (American Council on Education 1988; *Economist* 1990a).

Projections of changing demographic profiles nationwide indicate that nearly 12 percent of the country's labor force between the ages of 25 and 54 will, by 2000, be African-American, 10 percent will be Hispanic, and another 4 percent will include Asians and American Indians. Combined, 26 percent of the nation's workers in their peak productive years will be people from ethnic and racial minorities (U.S. Dept. of Labor 1990b). The continuing neglect in minority education has a potential economic effect in light of differential fertility by class, ethnicity, and region. If this level of education and professional preparation continues, a shortage of qualified workers who can satisfy the demands of the market will soon occur (Hodgkinson 1983).

In addition, enrollment at institutions of higher education has slowed in recent years, and in most states, the number of high school graduates is declining (Hodgkinson 1986; U.S. Dept. of Education 1989). These facts, coupled with the economic realities of our times, have created a financial squeeze that has brought largely untapped resources to the attention of college and university administrators. For all these reasons—social, moral, and economic—the issue of recruiting more minority students into higher education remains an urgent priority.

Of course, no single measure can solve the problem of minority undereducation, and higher education institutions cannot and should not have to do it alone. Much, however, is within their purview. Bringing more minority students to college campuses is clearly one important step, and therefore recruitment is an essential part of any successful institutional plan for increasing minorities' participation. It is only the beginning, however. Ensuring academic success and graduating are the necessary complements to achieving equity in education.

Colleges and universities have developed strategies for recruiting students to offset their low enrollment, but these programs often do not include responses to the specific requirements of the minority community (Christoffel 1986). Even institutions with the best intentions begin recruitment by arranging appointments at high schools with little or no preparation and then proceed to speak to large groups of students about the standard academic and social advantages of pursuing a degree at their institution. With this approach, however, a whole range of questions remains unanswered, and consequently results are achieved largely by chance. To be meaningful, recruitment of minority students should be part of a more holistic and systemic approach that also embraces the goals of access and retention.

Recruiting minority students is naturally complex because it is related so intricately to these other educational concerns. It is also complex, however, because of a more fundamental matter: the identity of the population in question. Although we use the term "minorities," no such single group of people fits the term, certainly not in the sense of common origin or cultural unity or shared language. Each group should be recognized and respected for the individuality of its history, culture, and language. The problems that confront different minority groups sometimes vary, and the practices employed to address them should naturally correspond when possible. The circumstances that limit the access and success of people of color in higher education are similar, however. In discussing these common issues, we have used the term "minorities," aware of the limitations it imposes. This report discusses four principal ethnic and racial minority groups: African-American, Hispanic, Asian-American, and American Indian.

While most of the factors that limit participation in higher education affect all groups, they do so to a greater or lesser extent, and the measures required to overcome the various obstacles may differ from one group to another. The case of dropping out of high school is an example. The smaller pool of high school graduates is a critical factor for both Hispanics and African-Americans, but for Hispanics, the problem begins in the transition from eighth grade to high school, a phenomenon that does not apply to the same extent with regard to other minority groups. This particular phenomenon is more evident for Puerto Ricans than it is for Cubans. When discussing the recruitment of minority students, therefore, it is important not only to analyze the different circumstances that exist for minorities in relation to the majority population, but also to consider carefully the differences that exist within the various minority groups (Monsivais and Bustillos 1990).

Examining the subgroups within each ethnic group also helps define the population of racial and ethnic "minorities." Because the proportion of students in higher education from the Asian/Pacific Islander population more than represents the proportion of that population in general society, most of the literature on "underrepresented minorities" no longer includes Asians. The literature indicates, however, that Pacific Islanders (Filipinos, for example) and Southeast Asians do not have the same socioeconomic or educational profile as other Asian groups and are indeed underrepresented on college campuses.

Throughout this report, the recruitment of minority students is discussed with reference to the most homogeneous groups of people feasible. Because studies are reported in the literature to a large extent based on aggregate data, however, the degree to which this application has been possible is limited. In discussions concerning recruitment in the larger context, minorities have been referred to in general as a population distinct from nonminorities. In chapters that discuss educational factors or cultural characteristics that may differ for various groups, distinctions are made wherever possible.

In addition to reading the literature, the authors, in the interest of producing a complete and accurate report, have conducted personal interviews, visited community organizations, and explored minority networks at various educational institutions.

HISTORICAL BACKGROUND

The practice of recruiting minority students in higher education is largely a response to the landmark Supreme Court decisions and the federal legislation and education policy of the civil rights era (Arvizu and Arciniega 1985; Galligani 1984). Since its inception, however, the purpose of minority recruitment and its terms, methods, and effects have evolved substantially.

Initial Efforts

In 1950, over 90 percent of African-American students were educated in traditionally black colleges. By 1954, with the Supreme Court decision in *Brown* v. *Board of Education,* such racial segregation in public education was declared illegal (Fleming 1984). Subsequently, substantial numbers of African-American students enrolled at previously all-white institutions (Turner 1980). In fact, by 1964, 114,000 African-American students were attending predominantly white institutions, most of which were located out of the South (Gurin and Epps 1975). The sweeping legislation of 1964, 1965, and 1968 further articulated and accentuated the new goal of racial integration in higher education (Green 1982; *N.Y. Times* 1988c; Van Alstyne 1978).

African-American students were expected "to blend into the sociocultural life of the campus. . . ."

The Civil Rights Act of 1964 "toughened means of federal enforcement against discriminatory use" of the increased federal funding to higher education institutions (Preer 1981, p. 3; see also Dunston et al. 1983). At the same time, the financial assistance provided by the Economic Opportunity Act of 1964 and the Higher Education Amendments of 1968 helped to turn access into a reality for many African-American students. Few colleges were responding to their needs and expectations, however (Ascher 1983; Fleming 1984). While administrators recognized that some change would follow, that change was expected to occur with little or no conflict (Peterson et al. 1979). African-American students were expected "to blend into the sociocultural life of the campus" and to compete academically, without any significant changes in the academic structure or in programs (Fleming 1984, p. 12). A survey sample of 1,168 institutions studied in the latter part of the 1960s reveals that 82 percent of colleges, in admitting African-American students, had either adopted open admissions policies or used special admissions criteria, but that only 50 percent provided special academic support programs and most of them made no effort to update their curricula (McDaniel and McKee 1971).

During this period, the main task of admissions offices was to sift through and evaluate college applications; students were still in large supply. According to some, the function of admissions was to make sure that the wrong people did not get into the school (Ingersoll 1988). The main purpose of the recruitment staff was college public relations. Recruiters provided information about admissions standards, described new programs and services, and attempted to attract qualified students to apply.

Not all the impetus for greater participation by minorities originated with the legislative body. The new political activism that characterized the late 1960s "generated a proliferation of black student organizations that expressed a need for black political and cultural identity. These organizations were instrumental in mobilizing the recruitment efforts that dramatically increased both the numbers and diversity of black students on all-white campuses in that decade" (Smith 1980, p. 29; see also Fleming 1984, pp. 11–12).

While talented students who met the merit criteria of high school grades and aptitude test scores benefited from the efforts initiated by both legislators and activists, a much larger number of academically and economically disadvantaged students remained shut out of the system (Rossmann et al. 1975). Even after the 1954 Supreme Court ruling to desegregate, some states continued to operate dual systems of higher education, and, as a consequence, the NAACP filed a lawsuit, referred to as the *Adams* case, against the Department of Health, Education, and Welfare, charging that the department's Office of Civil Rights had failed to take action against the education systems in those states. U.S. District Judge John H. Pratt ordered the Office of Civil Rights in 1973 to develop plans with the states to desegregate their systems of higher education (Jaschik 1987; Melendez and Wilson 1985).

Peak Years

Erupting social conflict and student unrest added to the pressures for broader and more flexible admissions. At institutions like The City University of New York (CUNY) and Virginia State University, the policy of open admissions, referred to by Clark Kerr as "the most important single development in higher education," was a result that revolutionized the mission of increasing minority participation (Rossmann et al. 1975).

In the case of CUNY, before 1970, both the two-year and four-year colleges had entrance requirements based on high school average or a combination of high school average and achievement test scores. Although the cutoff points varied somewhat from one college to another, in general students with averages of 80 or above were eligible to enroll in four-year programs. The two-year colleges required a high school average of 75 for entry to a transfer program, while students with high school averages below 75 but not lower than 70 were admitted only to two-year career programs. Students with averages below 70 or who had not taken an academic program in high school were not eligible to enroll in any college of CUNY. The special programs for disadvantaged students (through which most of the minorities at the university were enrolled) were an exception to this rule. With open admissions, the guidelines for entry to the four-year institutions were modified to include students who were in the top half of their graduating class or who had an average of 80 or above. All other students were then eligible to enroll at the two-year institutions (Rossmann et al. 1975).

The new policy opened the university's doors to a great number of people. While white students were the prime beneficiaries of the new policy, the proportion of African-American and Puerto Rican students attending the university increased substantially (Lavin 1974).

With recruitment not necessary in open-admissions institutions, the focus shifted to testing in the basic skills, placement, and counseling, and the new objectives of institutional reform became the implementation of compensatory programs for underprepared students, a new and controversial role for higher education.

In many instances, the special programs for economically and academically disadvantaged students were staffed by their own minority recruiters, and admissions offices often worked independently of the economic opportunity programs. Institutions of higher education were criticized for creating this dichotomy, as equal opportunity programs frequently became the sole source of recruiting minority students, resulting in the exclusion of minority students not economically or academically disadvantaged (Taddiken 1981).

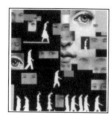

In other states, the response was manifested in other ways. The expansion of community colleges was seen as a way of addressing the needs of nontraditional students without compromising the standards of four-year institutions (Richardson 1988). Critics have argued that this two-tier system allowed the four-year colleges to evade the responsibility of recruiting minorities, relegating it to the two-year colleges (Cohen 1981; Olivas and Alimba 1979; Richardson 1988). The objective of recruiting minorities from two-year to four-year colleges was, to a large extent, never realized (Donovan and Schaier-Peleg 1988).

As social pressures from other groups began to be felt, the concept of "minority" in the public consciousness expanded to include Hispanics, Native Americans, and Asians, and the word "minority" was replaced with the term "racial and ethnic minorities." Changing attitudes were reflected in the literature, as agencies and individuals began to report on the various minority groups as separate populations: African-Americans, Hispanics, American Indians/Alaska Natives, and Asians/Pacific Islanders. Colleges and universities included these racial and ethnic subgroups in special programs and as part of their focus on minority recruitment, frequently with a special emphasis on women.

In the independent sector and in the selective public institutions, the approach to minority recruitment focused on the adoption of alternative criteria for admissions. In these cases, the weighting of admissions criteria, such as class rank, high school grades, SAT scores, and letters of recommendation, was modified to reflect more equitable consideration of minority students. Other institutions permitted admission only through special status. In such cases, committees reviewed a student's application and, based on strong letters of recommendation and a clearly demonstrated special talent, the committee would recommend acceptance of the minority student in question. Still others offered probationary or conditional admission to students not meeting the regular requirements for admission in which students had to complete prerequisite requirements, such as prefreshman summer residency programs, a basic skills sequence, and counseling (Halcon 1988; Trevino and Wise 1980). As with the public sector, active recruitment of minority students was still minimal; students sought admission to private colleges and universities, and enrollments were stable.

With the implementation of affirmative action through the admissions offices, many institutions sought to use a set-aside approach and to institute quotas. Reaction to the policy of using quotas for African-Americans and other minorities, however, resulted in the landmark Supreme Court rulings in *De Funis* v. *Odegaard* [416 U.S. 312 (1974)] and *Regents of the University of California* v. *Bakke* [438 U.S. 265 (1978)]. In *De Funis,* where Marco De Funis sought admission to law school, the Supreme Court ruled the case moot, but Justice Douglas, in the dissenting opinion, expressed concern about the cultural biases of a standardized test like the LSAT, biases that, he suggested, might severely limit the tests' utility in accurately predicting minority students' potential. He also expressed concern about the practice of reserving places in a law school class for select minorities (Astin, Fuller, and Green 1978; Cox 1979; Dunston et al. 1983; Hamilton 1979; Lincoln 1979; Preer 1981).

In *Bakke,* where Allan Bakke sought admission to the University of California at Berkeley Medical School, the Court was again divided. This time, Justices Brennan, White, Marshall, and Blackmun ruled that the use of race was admissible in university admissions, while Justices Stevens, Burger, Stewart, and Rehnquist decided that race was not an issue and ruled in favor of respondent Bakke. The compromise position of Justice Powell combined both views, concurring with the admission of Bakke to the medical school while supporting the use of race as a factor in university admissions (Preer 1981). This compromise position created ambivalence in higher education institutions in establishing alternative admissions criteria for minorities (Preer 1981) and resulted in a retreat from the momentum that was taking hold on college campuses in the recruitment of minority students (Atelsek and Gomberg 1978; Spratten 1979).

The students being admitted represented the two ends of the educational spectrum. At one end, the best and the brightest minority students who met all of the regular requirements for admission had achieved greater access and were being admitted where previously they would have been excluded. Others who were especially talented or who were able to secure special recommendations were also being accepted under alternative policies for admission. At the other end, economically and academically disadvantaged minority students were being accepted into special programs that had proliferated on college campuses, such as the state-sponsored educational opportunity programs. The students who still had limited access were the large number of students with average high school backgrounds. Depending on geographic region, the options for these students were two-year colleges or open-admissions institutions.

Declining Concern

As political pressure eased and new regulations governing the allocation of federal dollars were implemented, less attention was devoted to higher education for minorities. A study conducted at the University of Maryland during 1969 and 1976 documented an increase in median freshman African-American enrollments during the earlier years, immediately followed by a decline to initial 1969 levels in the North Central, Middle States, and Northwest regions, and decreases of 1 and 2 percentage points in the New England and Western regions after the peak year, 1973. Results also indicated a steady decline in the mean number of criteria for admission employed by institutions (Sedlacek and Webster 1978). The attitude that much had been accomplished in changing the complexion of our college campuses was perhaps what led to diminishing emphasis on the goal. Although overall college enrollments were stable in the 1970s, minority enrollments began to drop after 1974. By the end of the decade, focus on recruiting minorities had faded to near complacency.

Renewed Interest

As the college-going pool of students began to diminish in various regions of the country, concern focused not only on more aggressive public relations and recruiting but also on maintaining existing enrollments. Frequently, minority recruitment was accomplished only through special programs or through the efforts of a special recruiter for minorities. As long as cooperation and coordination existed among the various offices of an institution, recruitment could be effective. Many institutions, however, chose to bring together the previously disparate functions of recruitment, admissions, and retention, and presidents and chief executive officers began to realize the long-range planning importance of enrollment management for their institutions (Ingersoll 1988).

In the early 1980s, demographers began to warn of the impact that the decline in birthrates in the white population would have on college enrollments. At the same time, after the 1980 Census, demographers signaled the growing proportion of minorities in the general population and the shrinking proportion on college campuses. In response, recruitment took on a new face. A surplus of students no longer existed, and the vacuum was filled with the recruitment of nontraditional populations, such as part-time students and returning adults, and with the establishment of satellite campuses (Kelly 1989).

The renewed special emphasis on all of minority education—from recruitment to retention, graduation, and entry to graduate and professional schools—is now being fueled by a national concern for economic well-being. At individual institutions of higher education, the concern is also very real. As tuition costs soar, institutions are becoming more and more aggressive in their recruitment of minorities to fill otherwise empty seats.

Special Issues

Among the demographic literature, many researchers focus on the critical shortages apparent in science and technology (e.g., Dix 1987; Hodgkinson 1986; National Action Council 1988; Task Force 1988). Industry and government have expressed such serious concern over the projected shortages of college graduates prepared to enter scientific fields that it has been recognized as a national crisis (*Economist* 1990a; Naisbitt and Aburdene 1989), drawing attention to the severe underpreparedness of school students in mathematics and science, especially among minorities and women (National Research Council 1989). In higher education, institutions have begun to respond with incentives like partial or complete scholarships and special programs designed to attract students to these curricula. Recruiters are especially interested in students who are already prepared and who plan to enter these fields. One population that has been targeted to fill the void is Asian-Americans (Hodgkinson 1986). Indeed, a stereotype has emerged portraying Asian-American students as gifted, especially in math and science, valuing education, and having strong support from their families (Hsia and Hirano-Nakanishi 1988). Given the shortages in science and technology, and as a result of this positive image, some institutions have aggressively sought this population.

In recent years, two significant issues concerning the Asian community have surfaced. One is the distinction that has emerged between the application of the term "racial minority," which includes Asian-Americans, and "underrepresented minority," which does not. In higher education, the proportion of Asian-American students actually exceeds the proportion of Asian-Americans in the general society, and, as a result, some writers have questioned the need to include that group, even though it is a racial minority (Pemberton 1988; Ross 1986). It is clear, however, that certain subgroups of Asian-Americans, such as Southeast Asians and Filipinos, in fact are not represented in higher education equal to their numbers in the population as a whole and are frequently economically and academically disadvantaged (Hsia and Hirano-Nakanishi 1988).

The second issue, also stemming from a high degree of participation in higher education, is the question of restricted enrollments, or quotas (Reynolds 1988; Suzuki 1989). In the interest of achieving a more "substantively, culturally, racially, and ethnically diverse" student body (Hoachlander and Brown 1989, p. 11), colleges and universities have moved away from using strict meritocratic admissions criteria based on high school grades and test scores to including subjective and non-academic criteria. Authors argue that these policies are discriminatory in that they limit Asian-Americans' access to high-quality education and that they result from a manifestation of an anti-Asian bias (Reynolds 1988; Wang 1988). Asian-American high school students commonly maintain above-average grades and rank in class and score among the highest on standardized achievement tests (Hsia and Hirano-Nakanishi 1988). It is argued they should be admitted before others who have exhibited less academic achievement, without consideration of more subjective measures (Farrell 1989; Hsia and Hirano-Nakanishi 1988; Reynolds 1988; Wang 1988).

DEMOGRAPHICS AND DIVERSITY: What Colleges Should Know

Concern over the faltering pace of minorities' advancement in society in general and in education in particular has been expressed in recent years with conviction and eloquence. According to practically every measure of participation and well-being in our society, in education as well as in general prosperity, disparities persist between minority and non-minority people (Frank H. Rhodes, cited in American Council on Education 1988, p. vii). Individual institutions of higher education have a responsibility, to themselves as members of the academy and ultimately to the society it serves, to know and understand the realities that obstruct a growing segment of our population from full participation. The statistics in this section provide the foundation for examining the social, economic, and educational conditions concerning people of color in the United States as we enter the 1990s.

Population Trends, Socioeconomic Status, And Geographic Distribution

During the past 20 years, the proportion of minorities in the general population has increased so sharply as to "ensure future changes in the population balance between Anglo-Americans and minorities" *(Oxford Analytica* 1986, p. 35). This change is largely the result of two factors: immigration and higher birthrates. Immigration is higher than at any time since before 1920 (Robey 1985).

> *American immigration continues to flow at a rate unknown elsewhere in the world. The U.S., with 5 percent of the world's population, takes about 50 percent of its international migrants, not counting refugees (Oxford Analytica 1986, p. 20).*

Because most immigrants who have arrived in the United States since 1970 (77 percent by the end of the 1970s) have been people of color *(Oxford Analytica* 1986, p. 21), immigration is a significant factor in the discussion of minorities in higher education. Immigration is changing the racial fabric of the United States. In the 1950s, about 50 percent of U.S. immigrants came from Europe. During the 1970s, only 18 percent came from Europe, while more than 33 percent came from Asia and 30 percent from Latin American countries (Robey 1985). Immigration phenomena vary for the two groups relevant to this review, Asians/Pacific Islanders and Hispanics.

By 2000, racial and ethnic minorities will make up nearly 30 percent of the U.S. population.

Birthrates within the African-American and Hispanic populations are higher than in the white community. A summary of the size of population groups by race and ethnicity in 1980 and projected into 1990 and 2000 appears in table 1, indicating the growth expected in the minority populations. By 2000, racial and ethnic minorities will make up nearly 30 percent of the U.S. population.

TABLE 1

U.S. POPULATION BY RACE AND ETHNICITY
(Percent)

	1980	1990	2000
		Projected	
Total Population (Millions)	226.5	250.4	268.3
Hispanics	6.4%	7.9%	11.7%
African-Americans	11.7	12.5	13.4
Asians/Pacific Islanders	1.5	2.6	3.7
American Indians/Native Alaskans	0.6	*	*
Whites	80.1	76.2	73.2

Figures for 1980 for whites arrived at by subtracting "other races"; projections for 1990 and 2000 for whites arrived at by subtracting "Spanish origin." Columns of projected figures include estimates from different sources and do not total 100.

* = Not available.

Sources: Hsia and Hirano-Nakanishi 1989; Mingle 1987; U.S. Bureau of the Census 1980a, 1980b, 1980c.

The general decline in the number of school-age children that is expected to continue through the middle of this decade is not evenly reflected in all parts of the country. Because regional demographics vary, national figures can often mask major differences in states. From 1970 to 1980, public school enrollments decreased 13 percent nationwide. But in 12 Sunbelt states, enrollments increased, while many Frostbelt states decreased up to 25 percent (Hodgkinson 1983, 1986).

The high-growth states are also those with the lowest levels of high school retention: To a significant extent, students in these states are poor, handicapped, and of minority backgrounds, and speak limited English (Hodgkinson 1986). In other words, those states with the higher rates of high school retention will continue to experience diminishing numbers of students, while the states with the poorest records—those with high numbers of minorities, including students whose English is limited—will see bigger and bigger class sizes (see table 2).

TABLE 2

PROJECTED POPULATION OF 18- TO 24-YEAR-OLDS (000s)

Region	1990	2000
New England	1,369	1,185
Mideast	4,391	3,829
Southeast	6,344	6,238
Great Lakes	4,362	3,852
Plains	1,748	1,681
Southwest	2,672	2,814
Rocky Mountains	781	858
Far West	4,080	4,325

Source: American Council on Education 1989.

Regardless of student population, however, differential fertility ensures that the proportion of minority students in U.S. elementary schools will continue to grow. By the mid-1980s, "each of our 24 largest city school systems [had] a 'minority majority,' [and about] 27 percent of all public school students in the U.S. [came from racial and ethnic] minorities" (Hodgkinson 1986, p. 9).

The socioeconomic status of minorities in the United States is substantially lower than that of whites, as measured by several different factors. Median family income (discussed in detail for each ethnic group later in the section) is significantly lower for African-Americans and Hispanics, and the percentage of families living in poverty is several times higher. Families headed by a single female are three times more likely to live in poverty than are all families, and many more African-American and Hispanic families are headed by women alone. The most powerful statistic of all, however—and the one that perhaps has the greatest import for educators—is that *the single largest group of poor people in the United States is children.* Nearly 20 percent of all American children live below the poverty level (see figure 1): 14 percent of white children, 36 percent of Hispanic children, and 43 percent of African-American children (U.S. Bureau of the Census 1990c). Yet poverty rates decrease dramatically as years of school completed increase. The poverty rate in 1989 was nearly 20 percent for householders who had not completed high school, less than 9 percent for high school graduates without college, and under 4 percent for those with one or more years of college (U.S. Bureau of the Census 1990c).

FIGURE 1

PERCENT OF CHILDREN IN POVERTY IN 1989, BY RACIAL AND ETHNIC GROUP

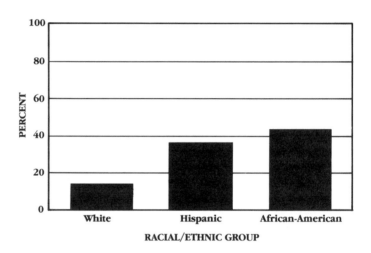

Source: U.S. Bureau of the Census 1990c.

Reporting on data from the early part of the 1980s, analysts have indicated two major trends affecting the geographic distribution of U.S. population in the 1990s: (1) the move away from the Northeast and North Central states to the South and the West; and (2) the move away from city centers to outer suburban and rural areas. In 1980, "for the first time in the history of the republic, the geographical center of the population crossed the Mississippi" *(Oxford Analytica* 1986, p. 42). This new migration notwithstanding, the East remains our most densely populated area: 80 percent of the U.S. population resides in the eastern half of the country (Hodgkinson 1986).

The African-American community

- African-Americans represent an increasing proportion of the population, but unemployment is higher for this group, especially among youth, than for any other group.
- Well over half of African-American children live with their mothers only, and 54 percent of families headed by African-American women with children under 18 years old live below the poverty level.
- Over half of all African-Americans lived in the South in 1980, and 81 percent lived in metropolitan areas.

Population trends. Although the fertility rate for African-Americans has fallen since the 1950s (*Oxford Analytica* 1986), it remains higher than that of the white community, and, as a group, African-Americans represent an increasing proportion of the population. In 1980, the total fertility rate (TFR) for African-Americans was 2.3, compared to 1.7 for whites. (A sustained TFR of about 2.1 is necessary to replace population. U.S. TFR has been below this level since 1971.) Though the number of African-Americans is increasing, circumstances deleterious to their greater social mobility continue to plague them.

Socioeconomic status. In 1989, median income was lower and unemployment was higher among African-Americans than for whites, Asians, or Hispanics (see figure 2). Median family income for African-Americans was $20,200, compared to $34,200 overall (U.S. Bureau of the Census 1990a), and unemployment was 11.4 percent, more than twice that of the total population (U.S. Dept. of Labor 1990a). Despite the gains made by some, African-Americans as a group are more likely to be unemployed today than a generation ago (Robey 1985). The unemployment gap between African-American youths and white youths was more than 20 percentage points in 1983, when nearly 50 percent of African-Americans between 16 and 19 years of age were unemployed. Considering that this age group accounts for a larger portion of the total African-American population than white youths do of the white population, the evident effect is that much more sobering (Robey 1985). Thirty percent of African-American families lived in poverty in 1989 (U.S. Bureau of the Census 1990c).

FIGURE 2

**MEDIAN FAMILY INCOME IN 1989,
BY RACIAL AND ETHNIC GROUP**

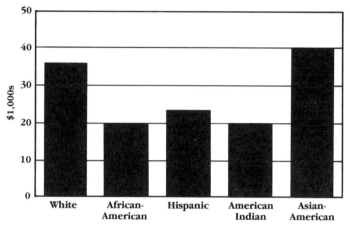

Source: U.S. Bureau of the Census 1990a.

In terms of its relation to socioeconomic status and ultimately to educational opportunity, one of the most compelling realities affecting African-Americans is the fact that so many families—more than three times as many African-American (44 percent) as white (13 percent)—are headed solely by women (U.S. Bureau of the Census 1990c). (The majority of African-American children—58 percent in 1984—live with their mother only [Robey 1985].) Because women continue to earn less than men do and single-parent families are more likely to live in poverty, the prevalence of this circumstance has devastating implications. In 1989, 54 percent of families headed by African-American women with children under 18 years old had incomes below the poverty level (U.S. Bureau of the Census 1990c) (see also figure 3).

Geographic distribution. For African-Americans, migration stems from the South, and their movement out of the South continued in increasing numbers until the 1970s. By the end of that decade, African-Americans started to move back to the South again, perhaps because of changing attitudes there after the Civil Rights movement and perhaps because of the general population shift to the South and West (Robey 1985). Of the nearly 26.5 million African-Americans counted in the 1980

FIGURE 3

PERCENTAGE LIVING IN POVERTY IN 1989, BY RACIAL AND ETHNIC GROUP

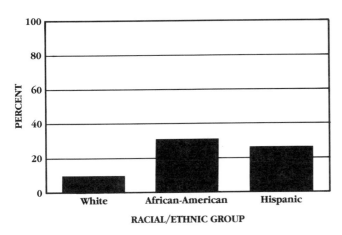

Source: U.S. Bureau of the Census 1990c.

Census, 53 percent lived in the South, 20 percent lived in the North Central states, 18.2 percent lived in the Northeast, and 8.7 percent lived in the West.

African-Americans have traditionally lived either in the rural South or in large city centers. Along with the trend for the general population, the number of African-Americans living in the inner cities declined somewhat (from 60 percent to 58 percent) between 1970 and 1980, and those living in city suburbs increased 43 percent. African-Americans are not moving as far away as whites, who are going to the outer suburbs and small towns, but they are settling in the "low-income inner suburbs" (Robey 1985, p. 149). Consequently, African-Americans are becoming a larger portion not only of central city residents but also of metropolitan residents. Eighty-one percent of African-Americans make their home in the metropolis. In many major cities, such as Washington, D.C., Atlanta, Detroit, Baltimore, Memphis, and St. Louis, they are or soon will be a majority.

The Hispanic community

• In the past decade, the number of Hispanics has increased dramatically in the United States; by 2000, they are expected to constitute nearly 12 percent of the population.

- The socioeconomic characteristics of Chicanos, Puerto Ricans, Cubans, and Central and South Americans vary substantially, and these differences are reflected in the degree of social integration and participation of each group in American society. Among Hispanics, Puerto Ricans have the lowest and Cuban-Americans the highest median incomes.
- Because of migration patterns, more Puerto Rican families are headed by women in the United States than are other Hispanic families, and the median income for these families is considerably lower than for families headed by women generally.
- Of Hispanic women heading households with children under 18 years old, 58 percent live below the poverty level.
- Hispanics reside mainly in cities and cluster regionally according to nationality: Most Mexican-Americans live in California and Texas, the majority of Cubans live in Florida, and Puerto Ricans live mainly in New York.

Population trends. Although the 1990 Census provides a breakdown of Hispanic subgroups, previous data collections do not. Until this time, the prevailing form of reference has therefore been to the Hispanic population in the aggregate. Between 1980 and 1988, the Hispanic population increased 34 percent, compared to 7 percent for non-Hispanics. About half of this growth resulted from natural increase (*Oxford Analytica* 1986). According to U.S. data, a 38 percent difference in births per 1,000 women exists between Hispanic (94 per 1,000) and non-Hispanic (68 per 1,000) women (U.S. Bureau of the Census 1989). "The age of the average Hispanic female is almost a decade younger than her white counterpart. With no increase in the fertility rate, Hispanics will increase their numbers of young Hispanic females" (Hodgkinson 1986, p. 9).

The remaining increase in the Hispanic population is the result of immigration. It is projected that "immigration and high Hispanic fertility will change America's racial and cultural composition, putting white non-Hispanics in a minority in some states early in the next century" (*Oxford Analytica* 1986, pp. 11–12). Population projections indicate a yearly growth rate of 4.7 percent, declining to 3.5 percent, resulting primarily at first from immigration and then from natural increase. Based on these rates, it is projected that the Hispanic population will exceed the African-American population in the early part of the next century (*Oxford Analytica* 1986, p. 37).

The major Hispanic subgroups include Chicanos (67 percent), Puerto Ricans (12.7 percent, not including the 1.5 million Puerto Ricans living in Puerto Rico), Central and South Americans (11.5 percent), and Cubans (5.3 percent). The remainder of the Hispanic population was counted in the 1980 Census as "other Hispanic." In terms of factors as significant as economic status, ability to speak English, family life, and demographic characteristics, the people of these four groups differ substantially. Although not much disaggregated data exist regarding Hispanics, some facts are available. The median age, for example, varies according to subgroup: For Mexican-Americans it is 21.9 years, compared to 30 years for Americans in general. More than one-third of both Mexican-Americans and Puerto Ricans are under age 15, compared to one-fourth of all Americans. This fact is significant because Mexican-Americans have a higher fertility rate than Hispanics in general. Cuban-Americans, on the other hand, have a median age of 38, and only 16 percent are under age 15, while 12 percent are 65 or older (U.S. Bureau of the Census 1980a).

Socioeconomic status. Because of different migration patterns, the family structure of Puerto Ricans varies from that of other Hispanics. More Puerto Rican women find work and reside in the United States than do men: 35 percent of all Puerto Rican families in the United States are maintained solely by women, compared to 15 percent of Cuban and 16 percent of Chicano families (Robey 1985). In 1989, 23 percent of all Hispanic families were headed solely by women. Of those with children under 18 years old, 58 percent lived below the poverty level.

The median family income for Hispanics in 1989 was much lower than for all U.S. families—$23,400, compared to $34,200 (U.S. Bureau of the Census 1990a). Income varied significantly, however, depending on Hispanic subgroup. Figures for one year earlier, 1988, indicate that median income for Cubans was $26,900, for Central and South Americans $23,700, for Mexican-Americans $21,000, and for Puerto Ricans $19,000 (U.S. Bureau of the Census 1990a). Unemployment rates corresponded, in that Puerto Ricans and Chicanos were unemployed at the highest rates (9.1 and 8.5, respectively, in 1989), while the Cuban and Central and South American rates were closer to 6 percent. These figures compare to 5.3 percent for the total U.S. population (U.S. Dept. of Labor 1990a). The percentages of families living below the poverty level also varied, although all were higher than for the general population: 31 percent of Puerto Ricans, 24 percent of Mexican-Americans, and 16 percent of Cubans and Central and South Americans lived in poverty in 1989, compared to 12.8 percent of all Americans (U.S. Bureau of the Census 1990b).

Geographic distribution. Even more than African-Americans, Hispanics live in cities, but the number of cities in which they are concentrated is fewer because they also congregate according to ethnic origin. California, Texas, and New York alone are home to 60 percent of the nation's Hispanic population. Three out of four Mexican-Americans live in California or Texas, 50 percent of Puerto Ricans live in New York (43 percent in New York City), and two out of three Cubans live in Florida (over 50 percent in the Miami metropolitan area). On the other hand, in much of the country Hispanics are rare: In 34 states, Hispanics make up less than 2 percent of the population. In major cities like Miami, Los Angeles, San Antonio, and New York, Hispanics make up, if not a majority, then a significant portion of the population. Metropolitan areas like Chicago, Houston, and San Francisco–Oakland count 350,000 to 600,000 Hispanics. In seven other metropolitan areas, Hispanics number at least 250,000 (Robey 1985).

The Asian and Pacific Islander communities
- By 1990, the largest Asian and Pacific Island subgroups were expected to be, in order, Filipinos, Chinese, and Southeast Asians.
- Although Asian-Americans are considered middle class in general, the socioeconomic status of the many Asian subpopulations actually varies enormously: Southeast Asians, the third largest group, averaged 50 percent living at poverty level in 1980, and 35 percent of all those in poverty were Vietnamese.
- The majority of Asian-Americans reside in the West, but large portions of some subpopulations are concentrated in other regions of the country, such as the Northeast and the Southeast. Almost all Asian-Americans live in metropolitan areas.

Population trends. From 1971 to 1980, Asian immigration totaled about 1.6 million, and from 1981 to 1988, 1.75 million (Hsia and Hirano-Nakanishi 1989). During the 1980s, Asians were the largest group of immigrants: A greater number of Asian immigrants came to the United States during the 1980s than were counted in the 1970 Census. These figures do not include over 500,000 refugees from Southeast Asia but do include Asian Indian immigrants, who previously had not been included in the Asian category. In the 1980 Census, 62 percent of U.S. Asians reported they were born elsewhere; their differing countries of origin are changing the face of the Asian-American community. Within the Asian population, the Chinese constituted 23.4 percent in 1980, followed by Filipinos (22.6 percent) and Japanese (20.7 percent). Koreans made up 10.3 percent of all Asians (U.S. Bureau of the Census 1980b). By 1990, however, Filipinos were projected to be the largest Asian-American group, followed by Chinese and Southeast Asians, who were expected to number more than 1 million (Hsia and Hirano-Nakanishi 1989). The Pacific Islander population is about 7 percent of the Asian and Pacific Islander group, and over two-thirds come from Hawaii. The median age for both Asian-Americans (28.8) and Pacific Islanders (23.1) is younger than for all Americans (30).

Socioeconomic status. The median family income of Asians and Pacific Islanders was $40,400, compared with the national median of $34,200 (U.S. Bureau of the Census 1990a). More detailed data are not available for 1989, but factors reported in 1982 based on the 1980 Census reveal that while income was higher among Asian-Americans than for the general population ($22,700 compared to $19,900), the proportion of families with three or more workers was also higher, 17 percent compared to 13 percent (U.S. Bureau of the Census 1980b). In 1980, vast differences also existed in socioeconomic status in the Asian/Pacific Island community. More than one-third of those in poverty (35 percent) were Vietnamese; in fact, Southeast Asians as a group averaged over 50 percent living at poverty level. For Samoans, the rate was also high, 29.5 percent. These figures compare to 7 percent for the Japanese and Filipinos (U.S. Bureau of the Census 1980b).

Geographic distribution. Similar to the other minorities described thus far, Asian-Americans cluster in urban areas and are about equally divided between central cities and their suburbs (U.S. Bureau of the Census 1980b). And, like Hispanics, Asians and Pacific Islanders congregate according to their ethnicity. Data from the 1980 Census indicate that over 80 percent of Japanese, 69 percent of Filipinos, and 53 percent of Chinese lived in the West and that proportionately more Asian Indians (34 percent) and Chinese (27 percent) lived in the Northeast than Asian-Americans in general (17 percent). Southeast Asians are found mostly in Texas, Louisiana, Northern Virginia, and California, where two-thirds live (Robey 1985).

For Asian-Americans as a group, 56 percent live in the West. California (35 percent), Hawaii (19 percent), and New York (9 percent) contain 60 percent of Asian-Americans. Illinois, New Jersey, Texas, and Washington have Asian-American populations of 100,000 or more.

The American Indian community

- The American Indian community is comparatively young and has more children than Americans in general.
- The large majority of American Indians do not live on reservations; in fact, most live in urban areas.
- While about half of all American Indians live in the West, every state contains American Indian communities. Many American Indians also live in the South and Midwest.
- Median income of American Indians is comparable to that of African-Americans and most Hispanics, which is about 40 percent less than the median income for whites.
- Compared to Americans in general, more than twice as many American Indians lived below the poverty level in 1980.

Population trends. The 1980 Census counted 1.4 million American Indians, about 0.5 percent of the overall population. The American Indian population is young, with 44 percent under 20 years of age, compared to 32 percent of Americans as a whole. Only 8 percent were 60 years or older, which is half the proportion for all Americans. The median age of American Indians was 22.9 years in 1980, considerably younger than the U.S. median age (30). At the same time, American Indians have higher fertility rates than the national norm. In 1980, about two-thirds of all American Indian families had children under 18, compared to one-half of U.S. families in general (U.S. Bureau of the Census 1980c).

About 500 American Indian tribes and bands were identified in the 1980 Census; about 90 percent of them, however, had populations of less than 10,000. The tribes with the largest populations (from about 160,000 to 235,000) were the Cherokee and Navajo, which together accounted for 27 percent of the entire Indian population. Other larger tribes included the Sioux (5 percent), Chippewa (5 percent), and Choctaw (4 percent) (U.S. Bureau of the Census 1980c).

Socioeconomic status. Median family income in 1989 for American Indians was much lower than for the nation as a whole, $20,000 compared to the U.S. median of $34,200 (U.S. Bureau of the Census 1990a). Like the case of Asian-Americans, the most recent detailed information available regarding American Indians is based on the 1980 Census. About one-fourth of all Indian families were maintained by women alone, and their median income in 1980 was $7,200, about 72 percent of the median for all American families headed by women ($9,960). The proportion of American Indians living below the official poverty level in 1980 was more than twice as high as that of the general population, about 28 percent of all American Indians compared to 12 percent of Americans in general (U.S. Bureau of the Census 1980c).

Geographic distribution. One-third of the American Indian population live on reservations (25 percent) and in the historic areas of Oklahoma (former reservations without established boundaries) (9 percent). While American Indians live in every state in the country, they are largely concentrated in the West, where almost 50 percent live in California, Oklahoma, Arizona, and New Mexico. The North Central region of the country is home to another nearly 20 percent. Of the 75 percent of Indians who live off the reservations, over 50 percent live in urban areas. Of the 10 states with the largest Indian population, only Michigan, North Carolina, and New York are east of the Mississippi River. About 27 percent of the American Indian population is in the South, 18 percent in the Midwest, and 6 percent in the Northeast (U.S. Bureau of the Census 1980c).

The Educational Profile of Ethnic and Racial Minorities
At virtually all transition points along the education continuum, disproportionately large numbers of minorities are

At virtually all transition points along the education continuum, disproportionately large numbers of minorities are lost. . . .

lost—at completion of high school, entry to college, completion of college, entry to graduate or professional school, and completion of graduate or professional school (Astin et al. 1982). This reality, within the context of the changing demographics of the country, poses a singular challenge to education.

The size of the cohort of high school graduates will continue to decline until 1998 (Hodgkinson 1983) as a result of the decline in birthrates after 1964 in the white middle class. Higher birthrates among minorities, however, have meant that minority populations will continue to make up an increasing proportion of college-age, if not college-ready, students. Further, the shrinking size of the college-age population is not uniform across the country: As a result of immigration and migration, the birthrate is rising in the Sunbelt states while declining in the North, indicating that higher education enrollments will continue to expand in one part of the country as they constrict in the other.

Most of the disparities in education affect all the ethnic and racial minority groups in general. Because disparities could be more or less severe for each group at different levels of education, however, it is useful to consider the participation and completion statistics for each group, organized by level of education rather than by racial and ethnic group. The following sections therefore discuss the rate of participation and completion for African-Americans, Hispanics, Asian-Americans, and American Indians (where available) relative to the rate for nonminorities for each educational level from high school through graduation from four-year college. Where available, trends in the rate at which each group obtains baccalaureate and advanced degrees and educational statistics comparing the public and private sectors are discussed.

High school completion

Each minority group exhibits important variations in high school completion rates compared to the white population. Hundreds of tables have been compiled on topics ranging from demographics to economic and enrollment trends to institutional finance and student aid (see, e.g., American Council on Education 1989). U.S. Census data on high school completion rates from 1974 to 1986 tell a discouraging story. After 12 years, and with almost as many setbacks as gains, high school completion rates for Hispanics and African-Americans are still much lower than the rate for the majority, especially when they are measured for students 18 and 19 years old. In this category, the difference in high school completion between African-Americans and whites is more than 11 percentage points (76.6 percent for whites and 65 percent for African-Americans) and between Hispanics and whites is almost 22 points (only 54.7 percent of Hispanics). By age 24, when 85.4 percent of whites have completed high school, the gap narrows to about 4 points difference between whites and African-Americans, but between Hispanics and whites it increases to almost 24 points, for only 61.6 percent of Hispanics in this age group have completed school (American Council on Education 1989).

In the two years after 1986, high school completion decreased for both groups (Carter and Wilson 1989). In 1988, African-Americans aged 18 to 24 completed high school at a rate of 75.1 percent (82.3 percent for whites), compared to 76.4 percent two years earlier. Despite the continuing disparity, however, until 1987 the high school completion rate for African-Americans was improving slowly but steadily. For Hispanics, the number of high school dropouts is disconcerting. In 1988, only 55.2 percent of 18- to 24-year-olds had finished high school, 4.7 percent fewer than in 1986 (see figure 4). Although rates have fluctuated, reaching a high of 62.8 in 1985, the most recent (1988) high school dropout rate for Hispanics is even lower than it was in 1976. The real school dropout rate for Hispanics is much higher than has been calculated, however, as a large number of Hispanic children never reach ninth grade and are therefore not counted in the high school attrition statistics (Fernandez 1989).

For American Indians, dropping out of high school is also a serious problem. The dropout rate for American Indians—35.5 percent—is similar to that for African-Americans. While American Indians represent 3.1 percent of all dropouts, they account for only 0.9 percent of all elementary and secondary students. Most American Indian students (82 percent) attend state-run public schools, while 11 percent are in schools funded by the Bureau of Indian Affairs and 7 percent attend private (many of them missionary) schools near reservations (O'Brien 1990).

Contrary to the situation for American Indians, Hispanics, and African-Americans, when viewed as a single group, Asian-Americans stay in school: In the 1980 High School and

FIGURE 4

HIGH SCHOOL COMPLETION RATE FOR
18- TO 24-YEAR-OLDS,
1976 VERSUS 1988

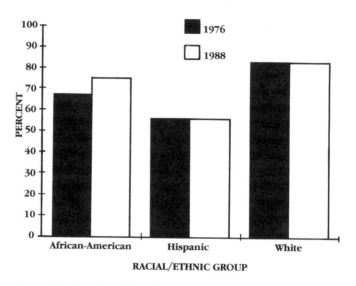

Source: American Council on Education 1989.

Beyond (HS&B) survey, the Asian-American group had the lowest high school dropout rate, the highest grade point averages (GPAs), the largest percentage of high school graduates who went directly to college, and the highest persistence rate at two-year colleges of any group, including whites (Hsia and Hirano-Nakanishi 1989). These achievements have been attributed to, among other things, a shared value among Asian-Americans in general of education, which is associated with status and respect and has long been considered a vehicle for social mobility (Hsia and Hirano-Nakanishi 1989). The sample used in the HS&B survey, however, did not allow for analysis by subgroups. Any differences among the various populations, therefore, would not be evident. While Pacific Islanders are frequently grouped together with Asians, some researchers maintain that their (Pacific Islander) situation in higher education is closer to that of other minorities (Bagasao 1989).

Other literature refers to state reports that Asian immigrants and refugees, especially those in the lower socioeconomic strata, are burdened by culture shock, limited English, and, in some cases, "a high incidence of violence and prejudice directed against [them]" (Tokuyama 1989, p. 69). Southeast Asians are reported to be falling into the at-risk category, with many not completing high school (Tokuyama 1989).[1]

Undergraduate participation

In absolute numbers, data from the National Center for Education Statistics indicate increases in 1988 college enrollment over 1976 for every ethnic and racial category. Nationally, college enrollment increased 13 percent for whites, 9 percent for African-Americans, 77 percent for Hispanics, 151 percent for Asian-Americans, and 22 percent for American Indians. More minorities are going to college, especially Asian-Americans and Hispanics. But given the variation in factors like population growth, the size of different age groups, and high school completion rates from one group to another, interpreting the significance of these numbers is complex.

For example, over the same 12-year period, the number of 18- to 24-year-old whites decreased 8 percent while high school completion rates remained the same. Yet, despite the smaller population, college participation increased 5 percentage points (see figure 5). Among African-Americans, however, the population in this age group increased 7.6 percent, high school graduation almost 8 percent. But out of this bigger population, a greater percentage of whom were high school graduates, a smaller proportion (5 percentage points fewer) enrolled in college. Among Hispanics, the same phenomenon is even more pronounced. The 18- to 24-year-old population increased fully 70 percent while high school completion stayed the same. Yet the percentage enrolling in college of this much bigger population, consisting of the same proportion of high school graduates, also decreased 5 percentage points (Carter and Wilson 1989). While the overall increases

1. Not all of the 20 or more ethnicities that comprise the Asian and Pacific Island community have had the same experiences in the United States, nor do they share the same degree of educational attainment. For example, the percent of 25-year-olds with a high school or college education was higher for five of the six Asian groups counted in the 1980 Census than for the average U.S. population, with the exception of the Vietnamese. Consequently, although aggregate figures provide an important overview of trends for Asians and Pacific Islanders as a whole, the gross numbers can obscure a less optimistic reality for certain subgroups, especially Filipinos, Southeast Asians, and other refugee groups.

in the number of minorities enrolled in college reflect important advances, they must be considered in light of the changes
in demographics. These data concerning the same 12-year
period seem to indicate that the number of 18- to 24-year-
old African-Americans and Hispanics enrolling in college has
increased. The number who do *not* enroll has increased even
more, however.

FIGURE 5

COLLEGE ENROLLMENT FOR 18- TO 24-YEAR-OLDS, 1976 VERSUS 1988

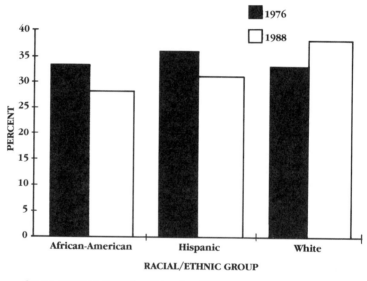

Source: American Council on Education 1989.

The college-going rate of young minority men in particular
has dropped significantly in recent years. College enrollments
among 18- to 24-year-old white men have increased 4 percentage points since 1976, to a little over 39 percent, but
among African-American men in the same age group, they
decreased more than 10 percentage points, to 25 percent.
Among Hispanic men, almost 31 percent of 18- to 24-year-
olds were enrolled in college in 1988, down more than 8 percentage points from 12 years earlier (Carter and Wilson 1989).

The difference in college participation between men and
women varies for different populations. Historically, more
Hispanic women graduate from high school than men. A

smaller percentage, however, enroll in college. The gap between men and women within the 18- to 24-year-old group in the 12 years from 1976 to 1988 has closed from a difference of almost 7 percentage points to about 1 point, but not because a greater proportion of women in this age group enrolled in college; it is the result instead of the relative decrease for men in the same age group (Carter and Wilson 1989). In absolute numbers of Hispanics enrolled in college, however, including *all* age groups, the number of Hispanic women grew 112 percent, compared to 48 percent for Hispanic men over the 12-year period (U.S. Dept. of Education 1989, updated 1990).

In the African-American community, the situation is a little different, but the general outcome in terms of gains for young women is the same. In the 18- to 24-year-old group, although a larger percentage of African-American women traditionally graduate from high school, 12 years ago a larger percentage of male high school graduates went to college than female high school graduates. This situation is now reversed: More African-American 18- to 24-year-old women enrolled in college in 1988 than men. The reversal, however, is the result of the precipitous drop in male enrollments rather than of any increase in the proportion of female enrollments. In fact, a smaller proportion of women in this age group enrolled in 1988 than in 1976 (Carter and Wilson 1989).

Two-year institutions. For all the minority groups and for whites, the proportion of two-year enrollments has increased in the past 10 years (U.S. Dept. of Education 1989, updated 1990). In the 10 years between 1976 and 1986, participation of African-Americans in two-year institutions decreased from 11 percent to 10 percent. For American Indians and Native Alaskans, enrollments remained virtually unchanged, at 1 percent. Hispanic participation increased somewhat, from 5.4 percent to 7.2 percent, and markedly for Asian-Americans, from 2 percent to 4 percent (U.S. Dept. of Education 1984, 1989, updated 1990).

In terms of proportional representation, it is clear that minorities are heavily concentrated in two-year schools. Of all Hispanic and American Indian students in college, the absolute majority are enrolled in community colleges. American Indians have the largest concentration of all minority groups, 56.6 percent, and Hispanics are similarly represented,

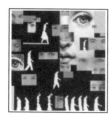

at 54.8 percent (Taylor 1983). Compared to the enrollment at two-year schools for white students (36 percent), African-Americans (43.1 percent) and Asian-Americans (42 percent) are also disproportionately represented (U.S. Dept. of Education 1984).

Data from 1984 providing a breakdown of minority participation by full-time versus part-time attendance indicate that two-year institutions have a larger part-time population than full-time population: For Hispanics, Asian-Americans, and American Indians, about two students attend part time for every one who attends full time, which is also the case for whites. For African-Americans, the difference is somewhat smaller, 58 percent part time and 42 percent full time (U.S. Dept. of Education 1984).

Four-year institutions. In four-year colleges, where participation of African-Americans has always been disproportionately low relative to the size of that population overall, participation also decreased over the same 10-year period, from 8.5 percent to 7.9 percent. Hispanic participation increased from 2.4 percent to 3.6 percent but remains significantly underrepresentative, as does participation of American Indians and Native Alaskans in four-year institutions, which remained unchanged at 0.5 percent (U.S. Dept. of Education 1989, updated 1990).

Of students attending college, a larger proportion of Asian-Americans (58.5 percent) and African-Americans (56.9 percent) attended four-year colleges in 1986. These percentages, however, are down 1.6 percent for both groups from 10 years earlier. A smaller proportion of Hispanic (45.2 percent) and American Indian and Native Alaskans (43.3 percent) attended four-year colleges. Among whites, attendance at four-year institutions was 63.9 percent of the college-going population (U.S. Dept. of Education 1989, updated 1990).

College completion in four-year institutions. The college completion rate at the bachelor's level varies enormously, depending on race and ethnicity. According to a 1986 study of 12,000 students, after six years of college, Hispanic students graduated at a rate of 20.4 percent and African-Americans at 23.9 percent, compared to Asian-Americans at 41.5 percent and whites at 43.9 percent. That is, African-Americans and Hispanics in four-year colleges and universities earned degrees after six years at about half the rate of white and Asian-American students (Porter 1989).[2]

Baccalaureate and advanced degrees obtained

Minorities as a group obtained more degrees at all levels in 1987 than they did in 1976, but when the data are examined according to subgroup, certain distinctions emerge. Hispanics, Asian-Americans, and American Indians made gains at all levels, and women made considerably more gains than men. But African-Americans, most particularly the men, lost ground: Fewer African-American men obtained degrees at any level in 1987 than in 1976 (Carter and Wilson 1989). From 1976 to 1987, the number of African-Americans earning bachelor's degrees fell 4.3 percent overall but 12.2 percent for men; the number of master's degrees decreased by 31.8 percent but by 34 percent for men. The number of Ph.D.s also declined 22.1 percent from 1978 to 1988, with a 46.7 percent drop among the men. While African-American women did obtain more degrees at the bachelor's, doctorate, and first professional levels, the number of master's degrees dropped 30 percent among African-American women between 1976 and 1987 (Carter and Wilson 1989).

While Hispanics are still seriously underrepresented among those receiving degrees—the percentage of Hispanic undergraduates (5.3 percent) is almost twice the percentage of those obtaining degrees (2.7 percent)—the number of degrees conferred to Hispanics over the period from 1976 to 1987 increased significantly (50.3 percent at the bachelor's level and 32.9 percent at the master's level); 52.8 percent more women and 16.1 percent more men earned a degree. For all degrees in this group, the percentage increases occurred largely among women; however, so few women earned advanced degrees in 1976 that even large increases result in relatively low numbers. For example, from 1978 to 1988, 25.6 percent more Hispanics earned doctorate degrees, 75 percent more women and 1.3 percent more men. In actual numbers, however, 273 doctorates were awarded to women, 321 to men. First professional degrees increased by 90.1 percent for Hispanics, for a total of 2,051 degrees; 748 were

2. It is also interesting to note that only a small portion of all students (a little more than 15 percent) graduated after four years, although this figure was about 12 points higher for students in the private sector (Porter 1989).

awarded to women (a 356 percent increase over 11 years earlier), 1,303 to men (42.4 percent more than in 1976).

The sharpest increases were among Asian-Americans, and, in keeping with the trend, women made the greatest advances. Between 1976 and 1987, bachelor's degrees awarded to this group increased 191.4 percent (215.3 percent among women), master's degrees 118.8 percent (121.1 percent for women); doctorates increased 56.9 percent between 1978 and 1988 (93 percent among women), and first professional degrees increased 24.9 percent (306.2 percent for women).

For American Indians in the same 11-year period, the number of degrees granted to women also increased to a great extent. Bachelor's degrees decreased 5 percent among men but increased 36.1 percent among women, master's degrees increased 21.3 percent among men and 65.9 percent among women, doctorates increased 51 percent for men and 42 percent for women, and first professional degrees increased 12.9 percent for men but 365.4 percent for women. In this group, however, the number of advanced degrees awarded is extremely small. In 1988, 93 doctorates were awarded to American Indians.

Public sector versus private sector

Private institutions continue to have more success in retaining and graduating students than do public institutions, but a recent report from the National Institute of Independent Colleges and Universities (Porter 1989) indicates that for African-American and Hispanic students, the advantage of the independent sector is not really much greater. In that study, the completion rate after six years at private institutions for African-Americans and Hispanics was approximately 30 percent, about half the rate for whites and Asian-Americans and only a few percentage points better than the completion rate for African-Americans and Hispanics at public institutions after the same period of time.

The proportion of white students in private institutions is greater than in public ones, although the figure has been slowly decreasing in recent years. In 1986, white students accounted for 81.3 percent of students at private institutions, compared to 78.8 percent at public colleges and universities, about 3 percentage points lower in each sector from 10 years earlier. The difference has been made up by increased enrollments, especially in public institutions, of Asian-Americans,

Hispanics, and nonresident aliens. African-American participation actually decreased in both private and public colleges
since 1976. Proportionately, African-Americans make up the
same part of the student population, within 0.1 percent, in
both the public and private sectors. Their representation in
the public sector, however, decreased 0.9 percent from 1976
to 1988. Hispanic enrollment in private institutions increased
from 2 to 3.2 percent between 1976 and 1988 and from 3.9
to 5.8 percent in public colleges. Asian-Americans made up
1.4 percent of private school students in 1976 and 3.2 percent
in 1988 but increased from 1.9 to 4 percent of students in
public institutions. American Indians and Native Alaskans accounted 0.4 percent of private and 0.8 percent of public students in each year, with no change in either sector in 12 years.

Summary

Disparities persist in high school completion rates between
whites on the one hand and African-Americans, Hispanics,
and American Indians on the other. While the gap has been
narrowing for African-Americans, African-American high school
completion rates have decreased in the past two years. The
high school completion rate for Hispanics fluctuates almost
from year to year. In the 12 years from 1976 to 1988, Hispanics
made only small gains and frequent losses. The 1988 rate was
slightly lower than that for 1986, and in 1988, close to half
of Hispanic 18- to 24-year-olds did not have a high school
diploma. The high school attrition rate is as high for American
Indians as for African-Americans. The overwhelming majority
of American Indians attend state-run public schools. As a
group, Asian-Americans complete high school at a higher rate
than whites. Large subgroups of the Asian-American community, however, especially Southeast Asians and Filipinos, do
not fit the educational profile of other Asian subgroups.

   While a growing proportion of white high school graduates
goes on to college, the proportion of African-American and
Hispanic high school graduates who go to college is shrinking. In 1988, the gap was even wider than it was 12 years earlier. Hispanic college enrollment has increased 77 percent
overall since 1976, 112 percent among women. Neither Hispanic nor African-American 18- to 24-year-old women are making real gains in college participation, however. Proportion-
ally, fewer of these women attended college in 1988 than
in 1976.

*As a group,
Asian-
Americans
complete high
school at a
higher rate
than whites.*

The college-going segment of 18- to 24-year-old African-American and Hispanic men has been declining seriously: Only 25 percent of African-American men and 31 percent of Hispanic men enrolled in college in 1988, compared to 39 percent of white men in that age group. This difference is 14 percentage points greater for African-Americans and 8 percentage points greater for Hispanics than in 1976. Compared to whites, a much greater number of all minority groups attend community colleges as opposed to four-year colleges.

According to a recent study, only about half the number of Hispanics and African-Americans earned bachelor's degrees after six years than did whites or Asian-Americans. Contrary to the gains made by Hispanics, Asians, and American Indians in obtaining degrees at all levels, fewer African-Americans obtained degrees in 1987 than they did in 1976. Hispanic, Asian-American, and American Indian women have made great gains since 1976 in obtaining all levels of degrees, from bachelor's through first professional. The actual numbers, however, remain very low. African-American women have made some gains in doctorates and first professional degrees since 1976 but only a very modest gain (1.7 percent) in baccalaureate degrees; the number of master's degrees obtained by African-American women dropped considerably.

Private colleges and universities retain and graduate more students in general than public institutions. African-Americans and Hispanics in private colleges and universities benefit only slightly from the advantage of the private institutions in this regard. The completion rate at private institutions for these two groups is only a few percentage points higher than the completion rate for the same groups at public colleges and universities. The proportional representation of American Indians and Native Alaskans did not increase in public or private colleges in the 12 years from 1976 to 1988.

INSTITUTIONAL COMMITMENT

The Role of Leadership

Leadership from the top is the driving force behind institutional change. Inspiring leaders are "dynamic, flexible, and precise—able to work with people, anticipate and accommodate change, and make decisions" (Fast 1977, p. 38); they look to the future (Fantini 1981), but "what is expected of them . . . is that they provide institutions with leadership appropriate to the times" (Murphy 1984, p. 443). A more ethnically and racially diverse campus environment begins with the commitment to this goal by the institution's governing board and the college president. In higher education, as in government or industry, it is the institution's leadership that must provide the challenge as well as the energy and the direction to meet it. Dedicated individuals among the faculty, staff, and administration can have a profound effect on the lives of individual students, but their influence is limited to the sphere in which they work. Achieving cultural diversity through the presence on campus of people from different backgrounds demands an institutionwide commitment (Arvizu and Arciniega 1985; Kelly 1989; Navarro 1985). This fundamental commitment must be expressed in the institution's mission statement. The development of a mission statement, although often expressed in broad terms, should include the concepts of diversity and cultural pluralism in a way that does not relegate them to the periphery.

The goal of bringing people of color to the campus is communicated to the trustees, faculty, staff, and students through the president's actions and words. It is the college president's demonstrated personal belief in the goal of cultural pluralism that will set the tone and send the message that minorities are welcome (Cole 1990; Rivera 1986; Wilson 1986). Effective leadership requires passion (Bennis 1990): On no issue will passion be more necessary or effective than on the issue of achieving a culturally diverse environment on campus.

A holistic approach to creating this environment includes relating the functions of minority recruitment, admissions, and retention with a diverse curriculum and an open, tolerant campus ethos. The tendency to view recruitment as a separate, isolated function at the institution is limiting, because the institution's policies regarding admissions and retention directly affect the function of recruiting minority students (Lenning, Beal, and Sauer 1980).

Recruiting minority students to college campuses and providing the mechanisms to support their success involves no mystery. The basic ingredient is institutional commitment (Christoffel 1986; Guichard and Cepeda 1986). If colleges and universities wish to include people of color in the college community, they need to set that goal as a priority and allocate the resources required to accomplish it (Halcon 1988). Having said so, however, it remains clear that the matter is not so simple. In many cases, it calls for a reordering of priorities and a redistribution of existing resources. In any community, change—and especially social change—requires courage and vision. "Effective leaders exude confidence in their own abilities and engender confidence in others. . . . They lead with their eyes focused on the future, working long hours to improve higher education in general, and society in particular" (Fisher, Tach, and Wheeler 1988, p. 19). Once the vision has been transformed into a community goal, the institution is in a better position to develop the programs, services, and people to achieve it.

While no single measure can solve the problem of minority undereducation, and higher education institutions cannot and should not have to do it alone, much remains within their purview. Given the enormous complexity of the problem, a college's responses need to be diverse. An institution's commitment is expressed in its support of minorities from recruitment through graduation.

Recruitment in the Institutional Structure
The collegewide perception of the importance of recruiting minority students depends on recruitment's place in the institution's organizational structure. Because organizational structures and perceptions of the location of power and authority within those structures vary, it is difficult to generalize about the optimum place for minority recruitment. One thing is true, however: the more authority vested in the administration that oversees minority recruitment, the more likely that the matter will be perceived as a priority. Further, the more direct the reporting line to a senior administrator, the greater the perception that leadership is committed to the issue.

Institutions of higher education have adopted a variety of approaches to recruiting minorities. The most common location for this function is in the admissions office, where two conflicting philosophies have developed. One is the belief that the responsibility for recruiting minority students should be shared by all individuals in the admissions office, regardless of race or ethnicity. Supporters of this position argue that if nonminority individuals are included in the effort, the issue will move from being a minority-centered concern to one of interest to the whole college. The other point of view holds that only minority role models should recruit minority students, because it has been documented extensively that minority students in fact respond more readily to people with whom they can identify (Rodriguez 1982). Accommodations to these conflicting positions have been made in varying degrees.

On some college campuses, minority students are recruited through special minority recruitment offices, which sometimes are staffed by a single recruiter. The extent of the institution's commitment to increasing the number of minority students is expressed in the size and physical location of and budget allocated to that office. On campuses where no other minority centers exist, the minority recruitment office often becomes a magnet where minority students congregate and where minority concerns are addressed.

Special support programs established with state and federal funding for economically and educationally disadvantaged students have historically been involved in recruiting minority students. Because large numbers of minority students enter colleges through these programs, they frequently become the sole avenue through which minority students are recruited (Commission on California 1983). In these cases, although minority students might also enter through regular admissions, no other special recruitment efforts are employed, and, as a result, the large number of minority students accepted to these colleges are educationally disadvantaged.

In response to social and political pressures, many campuses established the equivalent of an office of minority affairs to address such matters as cultural awareness and student leadership and to serve as advocates for minority concerns. Increasing the presence of minorities on campus in some cases became a natural outgrowth of these offices, formally or informally.

Often no special minority recruitment exists on campuses; rather, minority students enroll through programs and offices that were not designed specifically for this purpose. In these cases, coordination and communication among the various

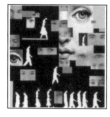

offices are critical to realizing the goal of increasing the number of minority students.

The Recruitment Team

Institutional commitment is also expressed in the moral support and financial resources given to those who will carry out the task of recruiting minority students to the college (Commission on California 1983). By setting the activity on center stage and arming those responsible with sufficient financial backing, the president can demonstrate the priority of the commitment invested in this goal. On the other hand, in institutions where the responsibility rests with a single individual and that person has no authority to create policy, institute initiatives, or commit resources, it will be clear that no real institutional commitment has been made.

Among the various people participating in recruitment of minorities, minority faculty have been central. Although most campuses have a limited number of minority faculty, historically, because of their personal commitment to people of color, many of these individuals have taken an interest and been active in recruiting minority students to their colleges. While such dedication is commendable, it has become a double-edged sword: More minority students attend college, but voluntary personal interest frequently is transformed into an additional function they are expected to perform. Because the activity receives little recognition or reward, the time and energy it requires can jeopardize reappointment, tenure, and promotion. From the point of view of the goal, the outcome is limited because of the amount of time and energy faculty can spend on the activity.

In addition to isolated individuals in departments throughout the college, dedicated faculty in academic departments and programs offering majors, minors, concentrations, and courses in areas like American Indian, Asian, African-American, Chicano, and Puerto Rican studies are also directly involved in recruiting students for their programs. Through these departments, faculty members can provide a direct line of entry to the college for minority students.

Staff and faculty involved in special support programs that serve disadvantaged students are also important advocates for minority students' participation. In some cases, in addition to teaching in and administering the programs, these people work closely with admissions and recruitment offices by participating in activities such as visiting schools, addressing minority students who visit the campus, and creating and maintaining networks in the community. Naturally, the degree to which they are involved in recruitment depends on the communication and coordination between the offices.

Some admissions and recruitment offices contain specific individuals who are responsible for recruiting minority students and who concentrate their efforts on locating and cultivating potential recruits. This function can be full time or part time, and it might be performed by one or more individuals in the office. Admissions and recruitment personnel establish links with the minority communities (Illinois Community College Board 1986), organize creative campus activities of interest to minority students, provide free transportation for school students to visit the college, set up information booths at schools and in public places, and write brochures and other literature tailored to students of different ethnic backgrounds (Bender and Blanco 1987; Warfield 1985).

All of the people discussed in this section can be effective as individuals and as members of a team. Even at those institutions where no formal office or specific individual has been identified solely to recruit minority students to the college, effective structures can be established to accomplish the goal. From a single individual to a heavily staffed administrative office, the types of mechanisms employed to recruit minority students are less important than the need for everyone to work as a team (Bender and Blanco 1987). Bringing individuals together who are responsible for and concerned about minority education in commissions, committees, or task forces is often the answer. Such groups allow all the constituencies of the college to participate, creating a collegewide effort and fostering a unity of purpose.

Respecting Diversity

One of the points most frequently raised in the literature on minority students is the propensity of institutions to treat everyone who is not white as a single group. The tendency to classify all people of color in the same category is powerful, encouraged perhaps by the nature of the bureaucracy in higher education and even larger institutions. Data collection, analysis, and report writing, for example, are simpler when fewer categories exist. The term "minority" does not represent a homogeneous group, however. The number and variability of the people included in the category make the definition, at best, imprecise.

As the campus presence of students from the larger minority groups increases, their desire to be recognized separately intensifies. In turn, the cultural identity of different nationalities within each group emerges to claim its place in the collectivity. The desire of Hispanics to be acknowledged separately from African-Americans or Asian-Americans is the same desire Chicanos feel in wanting to be acknowledged separately from Cubans, Dominicans, and Colombians.

In addition to differences stemming from cultural identity, other important factors affect the quality of a student's experience at the institution and directly affect persistence and graduation. One of these factors is social class (Astin et al. 1982). Regardless of the stereotypes that persist, all minority groups include people from all social classes. The same recruitment techniques and the same support services will not be effective in recruiting a middle-class Puerto Rican who was born and raised in Puerto Rico as in recruiting a Puerto Rican student who was born and raised in New York City.

Other important factors differentiate individual members within the group, such as cultural values affecting the role of women. The closely knit family structure in Hispanic and Asian cultures and the protective attitudes toward women make it necessary for colleges and universities to work not only with potential students, but also with their families if campus residency is a consideration.

Because of the differences between the Euro-American and Native American cultures, American Indian students may not be receptive to aggressive recruitment techniques; "hard-sell" recruitment may in fact be counterproductive.[*] Therefore, the participation of Native American recruiters is indicated as being critical for this population.[†]

African-American students who come from rural areas rather than urban centers are sometimes as different in their experiences as students of different nationalities. Their interaction with people and their form of communication, for example, could pose a social barrier in the opposing social context. An urban institution that recruits African-Americans from rural

[*]David White 1990, Salmon River High School, New York, personal interview; Minerva White 1990, State University of New York, personal interview.

[†]R. La France 1990, Cornell University, personal interview.

areas has an obligation to provide them with assistance in adjusting to an environment that might be far removed from their personal experience.

Immigration within the minority subgroups has been so great in recent years that it must be considered a distinguishing factor when recruiting Asian-Americans, African-Americans, and Hispanics. Newly arrived immigrants have different profiles from their American-born counterparts and others within the group. The new Asian immigration includes a large number of Southeast Asians who have less education and financial means than American-born Japanese or Chinese (Hsia and Hirano-Nakanishi 1989).

While in some cases the issues relating to recruitment are of concern to all minorities, in other cases, differing circumstances, needs, and obstacles identify issues specific to one or more groups that cannot be generalized to all. The reality, of course, is that both inter- and intragroup differences are significant, and recruitment must therefore be sensitive to individual circumstances.

A notable example of institutional leadership in the arena of creating diversity on campus and responding to the demographic changes in the state is the University of California at Berkeley, where attaining a pluralistic student body was an expressed goal. Between 1980 and 1989, the composition of the undergraduate population shifted from 66 to 45 percent white. In the 1990 freshman class, 34 percent of students are white, 30 percent are Asian-American, 22 percent are Chicano or Latino, and 7 percent are African-American (Magner 1990). Referring to the goal of diversity at the university, the president of the system, D.P. Gardner, expressed the university's purpose of "assuring that an entering freshman class is possessed of the kind of experience, potential, ethnic differences, social differences, rural and urban differences, and so [on] to enrich the whole learning environment and experience that these young people have . . ." (1987).

RECRUITMENT: A Collegewide Perspective

Recruiting more minority students into college brings with it the need to institute measures that address all of the reasons that relatively few minorities are on college campuses in the first place. Not only educational factors, but also social, economic, and political factors contribute to the exclusion of minorities from higher education. Because the problem of minority undereducation is so pervasive, recruitment in higher education is inextricably bound to the subjects of college access, admissions, and retention. Inadequate academic preparation affects all of these areas because so many minority high school graduates leave school less prepared than nonminorities (Smith 1980). Even if more aggressive recruitment were to succeed in enrolling all the minority students who meet the standard admissions criteria of most four-year colleges, the problem of severe disparities in higher education between minorities and nonminorities would persist: The proportion of minority students who attain that level of preparation is simply too small (Richardson 1988). Preparing students at the precollege level is critical if they are to be successful in college, and colleges have found that their direct involvement in this area has proved to be effective as part of both short-term and long-term strategies for recruitment (Wilbur et al. 1988). Widely recognized, nationally replicated models of programs that strengthen the academic preparation of students and prepare them for college include the University of Southern California's MESA program (Mathematics, Engineering, Science Achievement) and Middle College High School at LaGuardia Community College in New York, where a majority of graduating students go on to higher education, with many choosing to attend the sponsoring institution.

At the same time, for minority students as a group, the educational system breaks down regardless of academic ability or achievement. For example, high-ability African-American men drop out of college at a rate that is second only to the rate for the lowest ability group (Porter 1989). If institutions want to provide access and if cultural diversity is a serious goal, then colleges must remove all of the barriers that continue to obstruct the educational achievement of minorities. For most institutions, it will require a comprehensive policy involving admissions, recruitment, and retention (Christoffel 1986).

Preparing for Minority Recruitment

Much has been written about the "revolving door," in which minority students, once successfully recruited to college, find it impossible to succeed. Researchers emphasize the importance of relating policies and strategies for recruitment to initiatives for retention, as so many minority students are recruited into colleges and universities, only to leave within a matter of months. Factors affecting retention of minorities are reported abundantly in the literature, including academic preparation, financial need, and feelings of isolation and alienation as key examples. It is to the institution's advantage to use as much institutional data as possible to understand the reasons for students' premature departure before developing a comprehensive plan for recruitment; it makes no sense to recruit minority students if most of them will leave the college without degrees (Magner 1989). Determining whether problem areas exist in the institution with regard to minorities is the essential starting point.

A discussion of Tinto's model of student/institution fit (Pascarella 1986) emphasizes that the dynamics of students' persistence or withdrawal are unique to the particular institution. Both the variables that influence retention and the interventions designed to affect it "may not be generally applied from one institution to another" (p. 105). A coordinated program of research investigating minority students' enrollment and success and the ways in which recruitment is presently performed is the recommended first step in any recruitment plan (Pelletier and McNamera 1985; Wilson 1986).

Such an institutional audit (Green 1989) would include a student profile that not only separates the principal minority groups (African-American, Hispanic, Asian-American, American Indian), but also provides information on the various subgroups they comprise. The profile should include factors such as employment, part-time or full-time enrollment, socioeconomic background, background and proficiency in the English language, degree program, and academic preparation and performance. These data should be analyzed for the student body as a whole and for the entering freshman class in particular, as it will include all students before attrition. Similarly, a profile of the faculty, staff, and administrators by race and ethnicity is important to determine not only the number but also the rank and visibility of minority members.

While many aspects of minority recruitment will apply in all cases, any strategy undertaken should include a comprehensive understanding of the local situation, taking into account the institution's mission, the financial and human resources at its disposal for accomplishing the task, and an understanding of the complexities of the problem as it exists locally.

Recruitment and Admissions

A system of higher education based solely on merit excludes most people of color and has been charged as "the single most serious obstacle to the educational progress of disadvantaged minorities" (Astin et al. 1982, p. 154). Under such a system, the extent of change in the individual as a result of education, or its value-added benefit, is subverted in favor of screening for the best performers at the time of entry. Further, the widespread use of standardized testing in traditional admissions practices is "detrimental to the progress of minorities" (Astin et al. 1982, p. 157). According to a simulation survey conducted at the Higher Education Research Institute:

> When [college] application rates are so high that only one out of ten applicants can be admitted . . . a school relying solely on test scores to determine selection would admit only 1 percent of the black applicants and 3 percent of the Chicano applicants, compared to 10 percent of the white applicants. In other words, a white student is three times more likely to be selected than a Chicano student, . . . ten times more likely than a black student. . . . Clearly, if these minority groups are ever to approximate educational parity, some other approach to admissions must be found (Astin, Fuller, and Green 1978, pp. 162–63).

. . . the extent of change in the individual as a result of education . . . is subverted in favor of screening for the best performers at the time of entry.

Most admissions policies are grounded in the position that those students should be admitted who are most likely to succeed (Ascher 1983). Following from that position, the predictive measures of high school performance, reflected in high school grades and class rank and scores on standardized tests like the ACT and SAT, are widely used as indicators of future academic performance and persistence in college. These criteria are consequently the principal determinants in most institutions' decisions to accept or reject students for admission. Much of the discussion involving the use of alternative criteria for admissions disputes both the validity of these measures and their use to the exclusion of all other measures as predictors of success for minority students.

High school grades have been shown to predict college GPA for all groups, minorities and whites alike, but not to the same degree. High school grades as predictors of academic performance in college are less consistent for African-Americans, Chicanos, and Puerto Ricans than they are for American Indians and whites (Astin et al. 1982). Furthermore, standardized test scores do not contribute to the prediction of college grades for American Indians and Puerto Ricans, although they are shown to be predictive of college GPA for African-Americans and Chicanos (Astin et al. 1982). "The magnitude of the relationship [of test scores to college GPA, however,] is quite small in comparison to the relationship between high school grades and college grades" (p. 92). In defense of the validity of the SAT, "it consistently measures for all groups of students what it is designed to measure, without inherent disadvantage to any single minority group" (Hanford 1982, p. 3).

While the SAT is a reliable predictor of academic performance regardless of race or ethnicity, all of these variables—test scores, class rank, and high school grades—are related to socioeconomic status and parents' educational background (Ascher 1983). Consequently, minority students have less of a chance to do well. "The measurement of academic aptitude and achievement represents only one dimension of an individual's capacity for growth and education in the broadest understanding of that term" (Hanford 1982, p.14).

Using alternative criteria for admissions in the selection of minority students for entry to college provides an opportunity to weigh all admissions factors in relation to one another. Where deficits surface with the regard to the standard criteria, other measures that signal potential for success can in this way be equally considered (Fincher 1975; Martinez-Perez 1978).

Recruitment and Financial Aid

Although the minority participation problem cannot be solved with financial aid alone, it cannot be solved without it either (Hardesty 1990, p. 4).

One of the most frequently repeated observations in the literature regarding the decrease in minority students' participation in higher education is the unavailability of financial aid (Fields 1988; Green 1982; Jackson 1988). Studies concerning the impact of financial assistance on enrollment rates are as yet inconclusive, but "evidence suggests that financial need plays a part in admissions decisions and enrollments" and "denying financial aid to needy applicants does prevent those students from enrolling in higher education institutions" (Nora and Horvath 1989, p. 301). For minority students, the effect of financial assistance not only on enrollment rates but also on persistence is relevant if we are to understand the relationship of financial aid to minority students' attending college (Nora and Horvath 1989). Very little data are available regarding the effect of financial assistance on minority students' persistence; however, some studies (Astin 1975; Astin and Cross 1979; Nora 1987) suggest higher positive effects on persistence rates for minority students who received grants and campus-based aid.

Allocations for financial assistance have been severely reduced in the past decade. In the 1960s and 1970s, increased access and participation were expressed concerns, and the federal government responded by directing federal outlays to individual students through financial assistance. In 1975, student aid totaled 72 percent of federal spending in higher education. The importance of the government's financial aid for minority participation in higher education can be seen in the fact that much of the enrollment of minority students in public colleges was the result of federal initiatives and incentives, particularly financial aid programs (Green 1982). Since then, most of the government's financial aid initiatives that were instituted have been consistently and drastically cut back.

The rapidly escalating cost to attend college is a major factor in a student's decision to go to college. But at the same time costs are soaring, sources through which financial assistance is available are becoming more scarce, and those that are available have largely changed from nonrepayable grants and scholarships to loans (Hardesty 1990). A study of enrollment patterns in five major metropolitan areas links declining minority access to increasing costs and limited financial aid (Orfield and Paul 1988; see also Allen 1988 and Orfield 1988). Further, financial assistance is more and more awarded based

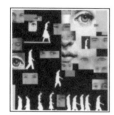

on academic achievement, leaving academically less prepared students with few options. For minority families already in difficult financial conditions, assuming the responsibility of paying back large college loans is simply not viable (Orfield 1988).

Other rationales also support the case for avoiding reliance solely, or even mostly, on loans for financing a college education. The type of aid and the make-up of the financial aid package students receive might also be important factors in both access and persistence. A study of the effects of financial aid on access to higher education concludes that financial aid packages that include a combination of grants, loans, and work appear to be more effective in promoting access than giving minority students loans as the only form of aid (St. John and Noell 1989). Studies have also indicated that students who receive diversified financial aid packages, including federal and state grants (Porter 1989) and work-study programs (Olivas 1986), are more likely to persist in college. It is also interesting to note that some minority groups hold cultural biases against borrowing (Thomas Mortenson, cited in Hardesty 1990).

While the principal barrier concerning financial aid is the lack of available funds, for many minority students, the first—and for some, insurmountable—obstacle is the process of applying for financial aid. The problem begins with access to basic information about what is available and how to apply for it. Often at a disadvantage in obtaining accurate and timely information, minority students can easily miss filing deadlines and therefore potential opportunities (Fields 1988; Olivas 1986). Advisers can help in compiling financial aid forms correctly and providing accurate information concerning the student's actual financial needs.

A financial aid adviser to American Indians in the New York area reports that many American Indians tend to shortchange themselves when filling out financial aid applications. One way is by reporting high hourly salaries for their parents without reporting that work is seasonal or that high commuting costs must be paid. Another common error is reporting ownership of one's home when the house is on Indian lands. Because such houses cannot be used to secure bank loans (Indian lands are held in trust by the federal government), they should not be counted among the family's assets, which contribute to the amount of parental contribution (Wiley

1989). Besides compiling accurate aid applications, another important consideration for American Indians concerns the schedules of federal, state, and tribal payments. Because the actual funds frequently arrive after tuition and other costs are due, students are unable to begin classes on schedule (Wiley 1989).

The rising costs of higher education have been cited as a major concern for most Americans. For people of color, three times as many of whom live below the poverty level, they are often the deciding factor in getting an education or not. Special programs focusing on financial aid can facilitate recruitment and are one way to bridge the gap. The Association for Loan Free Education assists low-income minority students with grants and counseling about financial aid in addition to its other academic and personal services (Hardesty 1990). At the University of Rochester in New York, undergraduate minority students are recruited to the university with a view to graduate school through an innovative program called "Fifth Year Free."* The financial incentive of tuition-free graduate study can be an alluring prospect for entering freshmen.

Recruitment and Retention

A study of student retention notes that the relationship between recruitment, admissions, and retention is a pertinent but, until recently, neglected phenomenon (Lenning, Beal, and Sauer 1980). Students are more likely to stay in college if they make informed decisions based on a sense of their personal and academic needs, on the one hand, and a knowledge of the institution and its programs, on the other. Postsecondary institutions need to provide students with adequate institutional and program information so that they can make decisions that will best allow their educational needs to be met.

Studies have shown that geographical region, institutional size, the setting (rural, urban, or suburban), school selectivity, and costs are some of the factors that count toward students' satisfaction and ultimately affect their chances of success (Astin 1975). For minority students, who may have special financial and academic requirements and interests related to diversity, elements like the ethnic mix of the student body and faculty, the availability of ethnic studies programs, the location of the school in relation to home, the availability of

*Dennis O'Brien 1988, personal communication.

special support programs and services, and provisions for financial assistance are especially important.

The objective of recruitment has been to enroll students in colleges with little concern as to the match, or fit, between the student and the institutional environment (Lenning, Beal, and Sauer 1980). Without an understanding of students' needs and the provision of programs and services that are responsive to them, however, the likelihood of retention is less than it could be.

Characteristics of students and the college environment that influence minority students' chances of staying or leaving include:

- Academic preparation before college (high school grades are an important predictor of college retention, much more so than standardized test scores);
- Good study habits and a college preparatory high school curriculum;
- Socioeconomic factors, such as parents' income and education, and the need to maintain a full-time job while in school;
- High self-ratings in academic ability;
- Relative youthfulness at the time of entering college;
- Attendance at an integrated high school (for African-Americans and Chicanos);
- Initial enrollment in a four-year college as opposed to a two-year college;
- A higher-quality institution;
- Financial aid, especially grants and scholarships;
- Residence on campus;
- Choice of field of study (for both minority and white students, better grades are achieved in the arts and humanities, social sciences, and education than in the natural sciences, engineering, and premedical curricula) (Astin et al. 1982, p. 178).

A survey of colleges and universities reports that different types of institutions identified negative characteristics of the campus in different ways (Beal and Noel 1979). In two-year public schools, conflict between classes and jobs was most important, but in four-year institutions, the most important factor was inadequate academic advising. Other studies support the contention that academic advising is an important factor in retaining students in college, in part because of the opportunity it provides for interaction with faculty and counselors (Astone, Nuñez-Wormack, and Smodlaka 1989; Glennin and Basley 1985; Mancini-Billson and Brooks-Terry 1987). The campus characteristic considered most important by all four campus types, however, was "a caring attitude of faculty and staff" (Beal and Noel 1979). For students prone to dropping out, almost all institutions reported low academic achievement and limited educational aspirations as their two most important characteristics (pp. 2, 9).

Other research defines the university as an enclosed social system with two subsystems, the academic and the social, into which students integrate and suggests that alienation from these subsystems contributes to dropping out (Langer 1987; Mallinckrodt and Sedlecek 1987; Nora 1987; Tinto 1987). A growing body of literature concerns retention as it is affected by noncognitive variables (Gosman et al. 1983; Pascarella and Chapman 1983; Pratt and Fedler 1982). While the quality of academic preparation has been shown to have the most frequent and significant relation to persistence, it is not the only variable that has proved to be important (Astin et al. 1982). For example, the incidence of academic dismissal represents only 20 percent of all dropouts nationally, and voluntary departure, despite a sufficient GPA, results from other factors, most importantly the "nature of individual social and academic experiences in college after entry" (Tinto 1989, p. 3).

The relative importance of academic, social, and economic factors in minorities' participation and success in college cannot yet be stated conclusively, but studies of attitude and perception also indicate that, in addition to academic preparation, several other factors bear on these students' chances for success. Feelings of social estrangement (Suen 1983) and sociocultural alienation experienced in feelings of cultural domination and ethnic isolation (Loo and Rolison 1986) are evident among minority students at predominantly white universities, and attrition may be just as much a function of them as of academic factors.

As a result, improving access and success in higher education requires a change not only in the students who are entering but also in the policies and practices of the institutions themselves (Astin et al. 1982).

Recruitment and Transfer

Much of the effort in recruiting minorities into postsecondary education has focused on increasing the number of students who make the transition from high school to college. A large pool of minority students already enrolled in community colleges, however, are an untapped resource for minority recruitment into four-year institutions (Sanders 1987). Disproportionately large numbers of minority students who go to college attend two-year schools (43 percent of all African-American undergraduates, 55 percent of Hispanics, and 57 percent of American Indians). Together, these students make up about 30 percent of community college enrollments (U.S. Dept. of Education 1989, updated 1990) and are the least likely to continue their education at four-year institutions (Crook and Lavin 1989; Orfield 1988). In Florida and California, where 76 and 85 percent, respectively, of all minority students begin their educations in two-year colleges, this reality is sobering (Commission on California 1983, 1985; Commission on Florida 1984).

Compounding the problem is the fact that minority students are not randomly distributed among two-year colleges; because most live in predominantly minority communities and commute to local colleges in their neighborhood, they are concentrated in a relatively small number of schools, where they make up more than half the enrollment. In fact, it has been suggested that the problem of transfers exists mainly at those institutions where most minority students enroll, that transfer is a "qualitatively and quantitatively different experience" in the two-year colleges attended by most minority students (Richardson 1988, p. 2; see also Commission on California 1985). The California community colleges with the highest population of African-American and Hispanic students transferred few, if any, students to the University of California (Orfield 1988). Furthermore, a study of community colleges in eight cities found that, in most cases, "minority students were less well represented among transfer cohorts than among community college students, and within community colleges, minority students were not proportionately represented in high-demand, selective programs . . ." (Richardson 1988, p. 3, citing Richardson and Bender 1987). In fact, according to the American Association of Community and Junior Colleges, about 35 percent of all two-year college students are enrolled in academic-transfer curricula, while the remainder are in vocational education programs.

Determining the actual number of students who transfer from two-year to four-year institutions poses a question that, according to some, is presently impossible to answer (Cohen 1987). The issue involves two principal problems: (1) The data referring to transfer are relatively scarce, and (2) the parameters for measuring transfer have not yet been firmly established. No generally accepted description of just what constitutes a transfer exists, and different institutions consequently use different definitions, inevitably resulting in diverse findings that are not strictly comparable (Cohen 1987, 1990). A precise definition has been proposed (Cohen 1990) that, if accepted, could prove to be an important step toward resolving the fundamental problem of inconsistent data. Making more data available, however, will depend on the willingness of higher education systems and individual institutions to recognize the importance of conducting such studies. Given the complexity of the issues surrounding the matter of transfer, this subject is one of the most important in the literature regarding minority students (Bender and Blanco 1987; Cohen 1987, 1990; Cole 1986; Olivas 1986; Rendón and Nora 1988; Richardson 1988).

One of the missions of community and junior colleges is to prepare students for the first two years of a baccalaureate degree (Cohen 1990; Velez and Javalgi 1987). The reasons few minority students actually succeed in transferring to and graduating from four-year institutions are varied. First, many minority students are not placed in academic transfer programs when they enroll in two-year community colleges. Low-income students especially, because of financial and family obligations, are faced with conditions that motivate them to choose vocational programs leading to more immediate job opportunities. A lack of adequate counseling and advisement precludes them from exploring other options and from possibly reordering their priorities (Olivas 1986). Being enrolled in an academic transfer track increases the likelihood of acquiring a bachelor's degree. Students at CUNY who were enrolled in a liberal arts curriculum, for example, were "substantially more likely" to obtain a baccalaureate degree than students enrolled in vocational programs (Crook and Lavin 1989). Second, minority students in two-year colleges are often academically unprepared for higher education as a result of inferior elementary and secondary school preparation,

Being enrolled in an academic transfer track increases the likelihood of acquiring a bachelor's degree.

which can result in low GPAs and prevent them, in many states, from entering four-year colleges. In other cases, although students might enroll in four-year programs, they encounter academic difficulty severe enough to cause them to drop out. Third, four-year colleges typically reserve few spaces for transfer students. Consequently, competition for these seats is strong, eliminating all but those with the highest GPAs (Nuñez-Wormack 1989). Fourth, even when admitted to a four-year college, many students discover that a significant number of credits earned at the two-year college are not accepted toward the four-year degree, translating into extra time, effort, and money beyond the expected two years to complete the baccalaureate degree and frequently resulting in attrition (Cole 1986).

Other researchers have investigated the problems surrounding transfer from different perspectives. Four principal obstacles to transferring for minority students include:

1. The poor communication of transfer requirements;
2. The lack of computerized data base systems coordinated with four-year institutions for the purposes of advising students on transferring;
3. Complex procedures for admissions and registration;
4. The lack of financial aid (Castillo 1984).

Hispanic and African-American students have reported unavailable financial aid as the most serious problem they face in transferring (Alvarez et al. 1984). At Mesa Community College in Arizona, over 94 percent of American Indian students expressed concern about financing their education (McIntosh et al. 1987).

A study using the data base from the National Longitudinal Survey investigated the effect on transfer of four predictors: personal background, academic processes, psychosocial process, and institutional integration (Velez and Javalgi 1987). Among the findings: Even for students with low socioeconomic status, the likelihood of transfer is high when the students also have high aspirations and good grades. Additionally, facilitating transfer to four-year colleges does not necessarily facilitate graduation.

Some state systems of higher education have instituted policies that address the problems of transferring. The Commission on Florida State Postsecondary Education, for example, created a policy in 1984 facilitating admission to four-year public colleges for students holding degrees from community colleges. Similar policies exist in other states, including New Jersey, California, and Michigan. These policies address questions regarding admission to senior colleges or the number of credits accepted. In Florida, Barry University and the University of Miami have considered the issue of credits lost during transfer. While admissions standards remain at these private four-year colleges, special agreements have been made stipulating that, for students who are admitted, all credits accumulated at the two-year college will be accepted (Cole 1986).

One stumbling block in developing articulation agreements between two-year and four-year colleges is that of curriculum. In many cases, the curriculum for the same major is different at the community college from the curriculum required at the senior college, resulting in students having to take substantial additional credits to complete the baccalaureate degree. Even when courses coincide, four-year colleges frequently do not accept all of the two-year credits because of factors related to standards and quality, also resulting in having to repeat credits. In another case, the four-year college might accept most of the two-year credits but assign them to the categories of electives and general education only, requiring the student to repeat completed courses in the major at the baccalaureate institution. One of the important areas in recruiting minority students is the development of articulation agreements that will overcome barriers related to curriculum, which so often discourage students from pursuing a baccalaureate degree.

Interinstitutional collaboration to effect better opportunities for transfer is also one of the key recommendations of a special report describing the recent emergence of a new kind of community college, the tribally controlled colleges of American Indians (Carnegie Foundation 1989). Twenty-four community colleges founded and controlled by American Indians and operating mostly in the North Central and northwestern states from Michigan to Washington offer a conventional college curriculum. At the same time, these institutions view Indian culture as their "curricular center." Reaffirming tribal traditions, these colleges also offer courses in native language, story-telling history, and arts.

*Beyond the classroom, traditional values also are embedded
in the very spirit of these institutions. Cooperation is valued,
for example. Respect for elders is encouraged. Differing
ideas about how time should be managed and how people
should interact with each other are understood and
accepted. In mainstream institutions, Indians find their own
values undermined; tribal colleges reinforce the values of
the Indian culture* (Carnegie Foundation 1989, p. 4).

In its recommendations, the report urges that connections
be strengthened between tribal colleges and non-Indian
higher education, especially through the transfer of credits
to four-year institutions and the development of cooperative
degree programs. Many successful collaborations between
tribal colleges and four-year colleges and universities have
been established, including Oglala Lakota College with the
University of Colorado, Black Hills State College with the University
of South Dakota, and Little Big Horn College with Montana
State University. Recruiting transfer students from tribal
colleges may be a successful strategy in itself. Evidence suggests
that students who complete their degree in a tribal college
and transfer to a non-Indian college are better prepared
socially and academically. According to a study at the Center
for Native American Studies at Montana State University, graduates
from tribal colleges "are at least twice as likely to succeed
in a non-Indian college as Indian students who did not
first study at a tribally controlled institution" (Carnegie Foundation
1989, pp. 77–78).

Responding to some of the problems of transferring for
minority students in general, other innovative recruitment
programs have been developed, such as joint admissions and
proactive transfer. In joint admissions programs, students are
accepted to both the two-year and the four-year institutions
simultaneously. Such is the case in a program between
LaGuardia Community College of CUNY and Vassar (Rodriguez
1988). In proactive transfer programs, a recruiter/counselor
from the four-year college, working with counselors
from the two-year college, identifies potential transfer students
in their first semester at the community college. These students
receive academic support services, enrichment activities,
and counseling, all sponsored by the four-year institution.
Such a program exists between Glassboro State College in
New Jersey and its feeder community colleges (Ryan 1986).

An interesting concept presented in the literature and responding to the finding that being enrolled in an academic transfer program increases the likelihood of transfer is that of a "transfer college" within a community college. Students participating in the transfer college would be exposed to close contact between students and faculty, peer support, networking opportunities, and the staff's high expectations, in addition to other benefits (Rendón and Nora 1988).

The difficulty surrounding the subject of minority students' transferring is couched in a complex set of circumstances involving all of higher education. Matters of curriculum, faculty resistance, state and local bureaucracies, and financial constraints pose real challenges to the higher education community. Some of these challenges are being addressed by state and national programs, such as the Exploratory Transfer Institute (ETI), a collaboration between the University of Arizona and Pima Community College. The mission of the institute is to encourage students of color who are not considering transfer to attend summer institutes at the university, exposing them to a world they might not otherwise have considered (Elvin and Wood 1989). Another initiative, a project of the United Negro College Fund, involves 16 universities and 10 community colleges in the South. According to the Fund, the institutions work together to increase the number of African-American students, in particular men, who receive baccalaureate degrees.

INSTITUTIONAL CLIMATE AND CAMPUS PLURALISM

*Pluralism is a euphemism camouflaging the deep-seated
conflicts that rage throughout the corridors of our economy,
beliefs, and values. And some of the conflicts that prevail
in the political arena originate on campus. The campus,
despite its frailties and inadequacies, continues to be the
major seedbed for next-generation ideas. Higher education,
in the splendid chaos of its courses and the wild array of
its activities, reflects the larger society and presages its future*
(Enarson 1984, p. 24).

For many minority students, college life is their first independent experience in a predominantly white environment. The
ethnic heterogeneity in society is not indicative of most
minority students' individual lives, because many minority
youth grow up in ethnic neighborhoods, attend mainly minority schools, and socialize with people of their own ethnic
backgrounds. The circle of family, friends, and community
before college is therefore one of social and cultural conti-
nuity. For these students, going to college can be a kind of
culture shock. One brief glance around the room at orientation can quickly sum up a new reality. Without any structures for support and inclusion, their feelings of isolation can
only intensify (Forni 1989; Smith 1980), as white students and
professors predominate in classrooms, and the courtyards,
cafeterias, and dormitories fill with others who are so much
like each other and so little like themselves. The transition
required, suddenly and not really by choice, is a difficult and
lonely one to make.

From the minority student's perspective, the climate of the
campus is made up of all the subtle and not so subtle ways
in which attitudes are expressed: the response with which
one is received in the cafeteria, at the bursar's office, and in
the bookstore; the degree of attention extended in the tutor-
ing center or in the classroom and library; whether or not
nonwhite culture is visibly reflected among the people, in
the curriculum, and in the social and cultural programs available. The quality of the campus climate and the degree to
which it is welcoming, indifferent, or openly hostile toward
a minority presence are not simple to measure.

Perceptions of whether or not a campus is hospitable to
minorities differ to an important extent between minority and
white students (Loo and Rolison 1986). Surveys at predominantly white campuses repeatedly indicate the disparity

between whites' and nonwhites' impressions of similar circumstances, which may lead to misconceptions of minority students' behaviors. Even though no incidents of overt racism are recorded on a campus, an inhospitable atmosphere could exist, affecting minority students' ability to cope and their determination to stay.

Curriculum

Colleges and universities are presently engaged in an intense debate over curricular reform that is of immediate interest to minority and Third World students. The subject is being discussed in all sectors—large prestigious research universities to local community colleges, conservative and liberal institutions, public and private institutions. Proponents of reform contend that the present curriculum excludes to a large extent the points of view of women and of minority cultures, while opponents argue that matters of race, ethnicity, and pluralism are inherent in classical inquiry, and reform is therefore unnecessary (Himmelfarb 1988).

Response to the issue of curricular change has taken a variety of forms and covers a wide spectrum. In some institutions, it has meant creating courses that focus on specific ethnic cultures (Zita 1988). This approach aims to educate students cross culturally, an objective that could be confounded when students elect only courses that focus on their own social or ethnic group (Olstad et al. 1983). Courses of this nature could be more or less effective, depending on whether or not they are included in the college's core curriculum as a requirement. Curricular change has also been instituted through the revision of the composition course, usually a college requirement, by using multicultural subject material about which students can read and write (Clark 1987).

At some institutions, such as the University of California at Berkeley, changing the curriculum has been viewed as one aspect of a broader initiative to infuse the principles of cultural pluralism throughout the culture of the university. In these instances, a major institutional effort has been made to "heighten faculty awareness of the historical, social-political, and ethical bases of their disciplines with respect to race, class, and gender" and to infuse these perspectives in courses throughout the curriculum (Nicholson et. al 1989, p. 1). At Rider College in New Jersey, a project of this nature included four main components: (1) a public symposium featuring recognized scholars that explored the various aspects of curricular integration, followed by workshops for participating faculty; (2) a collaboratively designed interdisciplinary course directly addressing the issues of race, class, and gender; (3) a faculty development program in which faculty from various fields each created annotated bibliographies and revised a course in their discipline to incorporate the issues in the stated areas; and (4) a focus group, in which eight African-American female students and four faculty and staff explored the issues of race and gender on the campus (Nicholson et al. 1989).

Reform has also taken place in teacher education. The National Council for the Accreditation of Teacher Education has recognized the need to prepare future teachers to understand the cultural backgrounds of the increasing number of racial and ethnic minority children they will be teaching, requiring teacher education programs to include a multicultural component as part of the teacher education curriculum (Bermingham et. al 1986). Again, the breadth and depth of a particular institution's response depends on the degree to which the underlying philosophy of multicultural education has been accepted (Grant 1983).

As colleges embrace the change and incorporate nonwestern perspectives in their curricula, a new dimension will be added to the criteria students consider when selecting an institution of higher learning. It seems evident that institutions that choose to include minority perspectives in the curriculum will be perceived as being more responsive, tolerant, and committed.

Critical Mass

Responding to a question about why she chose to attend a particular college, a young student put it succinctly: "There are other minorities there, so I don't have to feel like a Martian." . . . No matter how outstanding the academic institution, ethnic minority students can feel alienated if their ethnic representation on campus is small (Loo and Rolison 1986, pp. 69, 72).

In this context, the existence of a critical mass means having enough students around who are like oneself so as not to feel isolated, uncomfortable, and alone (Forni 1989; Smith 1980). One element in the nebulous concept of campus climate, critical mass is perhaps the most concrete, the simplest to understand. The term is usually applied with regard to the "comfort factor," the degree to which students feel as though they are part of the campus community as opposed to feeling like outsiders—alien, marginal, unimportant.

> *Being "the other" means feeling different; is awareness of being distinct; is consciousness of being dissimilar. It means being outside the game, outside the circle, outside the set* (Madrid 1988, p. 56).

It is easy to feel like an outsider to the community when the community is made up mostly of "others."

Feelings of discomfort stem from a variety of sources. The academic difficulty that many minority students experience can compound the feeling of not fitting in, making it doubly difficult to adjust (Green 1989). Knowing that others are around with whom to identify can facilitate adjustment, and seeing that other minority students have succeeded can affirm the value in the effort. The academic benefits and the effect on persistence of being among others of the same background may be significant. While the practice is not necessarily typical of or endemic to ethnic minorities, the strategy of forming study groups was shown to be a common and effective tool among one group for improving their academic success rate in a very challenging course (Teisman 1985). The presence in sufficient numbers of students from the same racial and ethnic background is clearly a prerequisite to forming ethnic support groups, whether they are academic, social, or personal.

As concrete as the concept of critical mass may be, it raises important questions with regard to the various ethnic subgroups embodied in the category of "minorities." Who is included in a critical mass for American Indians? Are they the same students with whom Chicanos will feel an affinity? Does the presence of African-American immigrants, from Nigeria or the Caribbean Islands, for example, increase the comfort factor for African-Americans at a predominantly white college? The group with which a person identifies is probably influenced by many factors besides ethnic origin. Only a few of them may be social class, duration of time in the United States, native language, and educational background. A Hawaiian student studying at Hunter College in New York, for example, in discussing her experience with other Asian students, noted:

In Hawaii, we never talked much to different Asian students. Most of my friends were "locals." At Hunter, you can meet first-generation students from Hong Kong and mainland China. Most of these students are from working class families. At first, I was surprised that, even though our backgrounds are different, we share a lot of common ground. I also understand better what these first-generation students have experienced (Bagasao 1989, p. 34).

Institutions with a genuine interest in understanding what constitutes an identity group for the various ethnic minorities on campus might consider investigating the question through surveys of the minority student population, counseling sessions, or informal small-group discussions.

Role Models

In general, minority students have not had much opportunity to see people from their own ethnic backgrounds in prestigious and authoritative positions in society. Students who are first in their families to go to college are not prepared for the demands and have nonspecific educational objectives as well as an "inadequate understanding of the relationship between higher education and career goals" (Richardson 1988, p. 6). The mere existence of minority faculty and staff who make decisions, provide direction, and influence policy within the college community can have a powerful effect on a young and impressionable mind. While most students are challenged and motivated enough when they arrive on campus, the daily routine, the unfamiliar responsibility of independence, and the constant demands of college can cause students to lose sight of the benefits a college education can bring. The presence of successful people of color can have a motivating, positive effect.

Minority students frequently seek out minority faculty role models for academic advice and counseling. Connecting with someone who can identify with their personal situation is felt to be important, and relationships are established either through the formal procedures or informal networks. At many colleges and universities, the benefit of creating links between students and faculty from the same ethnic background has been recognized as being instrumental in students' development and persistence. Faculty mentors act as friends, advisers, and confidants, and students accept them as people who

The presence of successful people of color can have a motivating, positive effect.

can show them the ropes because they have had similar experiences in similar circumstances.

Other important role models at the institution include administrators and staff, whom students may not see as regularly but who often provide valuable assistance. For many students, minority people in positions of leadership and influence are rare. More important, however, is the integration of values from other cultures into the institutional structure that minority administrators bring with them. A minority student who, for example, needs special intervention because of cultural obligations that conflict with a college responsibility may find himself or herself better understood by an administrator who understands and can communicate to others the values of his or her culture.

Whether a student consciously selects a campus because of the presence of people of color in the professional ranks is uncertain. The benefit role models provide, however, while perhaps not tangible, objective, or easily measured, is clear.

Programs Enhancing Diversity

If we have learned anything from our relationship with the Native American, it is that people cannot be torn from their cultural roots without harm (Nuss 1989–90, p. 3).

Ethnic studies programs
Clearly, the inclusion in the curriculum of ethnic studies programs is an indication to students that the institution supports them and their experience. The existence of academic programs in ethnic studies demonstrates the institution's recognition of their inherent value and affirms the experiences and perspectives of minority cultures on the world scene. For most minority students, the opportunity to learn about the history and culture of their ethnic heritage has been limited, as the curricula of most secondary schools is just beginning to reflect the diversity of cultures in America. Such a program in itself could be a strong attraction and an inducement to participate more actively in other areas of minority campus life and in campus life in general.

As noted earlier, minority students gravitate to programs and places where they can enjoy shared experience. The attraction of ethnic studies is therefore also a matter of people. An African-American studies program, for example, is sure to provide an environment where shared African-American experience will predominate. The professors and the students are likely to be African-American, the program of study personal and "relevant." For students whose native language is other than English, the additional attraction of dialogue in their native language will, at least in part, be possible.

Academic support programs

The literature is clear about the importance of academic support programs in developing students' basic skills and the impact that such programs can have on retention. For many students who enter the university underprepared, these programs provide the supplemental instruction needed to achieve and the emotional and psychological support needed to survive. The staff of tutoring/learning centers often become the persons with whom they can connect. Such individuals assist minority students in adjusting to college, meeting their academic responsibilities, and negotiating the system.

Students look for programs where they will feel welcome, and they gravitate to people who will listen and who care. It is frequently in these programs where they find refuge (West, Simpson, and Jones 1975). And minority students are quick to share these positive experiences with others in the college and in the community at large.

Social programs

Offering opportunities for minority students to join clubs and organizations that can provide academic enrichment as well as social rewards is important. For most students, belonging to a group that fosters and promotes their cultural or ethnic identity can be extremely gratifying. Such opportunities to meet with others like themselves are limited on campuses where few minorities are enrolled, and social activities can provide a stimulating way to meet new friends and establish helping relationships. Many organizations for minority students become involved in civic or community projects, which establish a kind of bridge between the old neighborhood and the new campus environment and allow them to return to their communities as "educated" persons who still care. On residential campuses where minority students are not able to go home for holidays because of financial constraints, friends become their bridge to a new extended family.

Social functions and artistic performances, including ethnic celebrations, such as festivals, theater, and dance, also play an important part in attracting minority students to campus. Opportunities for self-expression and cultural development are integral to personal fulfillment.

THE RECRUITMENT PLAN

Colleges and universities have developed a variety of innovative strategies for recruiting minority students. The key to effective recruitment, however, is not only in the strategies themselves, but also in the way they are incorporated into a larger design. Recruitment should therefore begin with the design of a plan. The type of recruitment plan a college develops depends on many factors: The institution's mission, the targeted minority groups, the abilities of the students to be recruited, and the resources allocated to do the job are only a few. And these factors are not mutually exclusive: The mission of the institution, for example, might delineate the range of abilities of the minority students it will plan to recruit. Given the wide array of characteristics of institutions across the nation, the scope and methods of each college's recruitment plan will vary.

Despite these variations, however, research has shown that a comprehensive plan will meet five basic conditions:

1. It will be culturally sensitive, demonstrating an awareness of the cultures of the various minority populations.
2. It will be based on a recent assessment of minority student enrollment.
3. It will be integrated with the institution's broader educational objectives.
4. Its objectives will be stated in terms that are sufficiently specific so as to permit a thorough and detailed evaluation.
5. It will be holistic, incorporating all the principal constituencies of the institution.

Developing the recruitment of minority students as a comprehensive institutional initiative requires a considerable investment of time. Setting up committees, collecting data, engaging participants in healthy debate, arriving at consensus are phases of development that could require years instead of months. In addition, the delicate work of encouraging key people to participate, sustaining a productive level of involvement, and drafting preliminary versions of the plan are essential to the process before a final plan is rendered and the institution is ready to move to implementation.

Basic Elements
Cultural awareness: The backbone
of minority recruitment

African-American, Chicano, Puerto Rican, Navajo, Mohawk, Vietnamese, Colombian, Filipino—the languages and cultural values of all these students vary greatly from mainstream America, and these differences must be understood and reflected in the design and implementation of the recruitment plan. Educators may be aware that minority students' language and culture are different from each other and from the majority, yet this reality has rarely been considered important enough to influence recruitment. Understanding the cultural values of the minority students the college wants to recruit might require a special effort, but it really is essential groundwork if these students are ever to become an integral part of the university (Green 1989; Madrid 1988). Many more students could be reached if the approach taken to recruit them were understanding of or, at the very least, not in conflict with their cultural values. The messages the institution conveys can present the college as a place students and their families can feel comfortable about or as a place where the environment seems alienating and unaccepting of their differences. Several categories of cultural characteristics are important to know about when formulating strategies for recruitment.

Family. Traditional cultures depend heavily on the support system provided by the family. Families are frequently extended, and the value of respect for elders both inside and outside the family is strong (Dupuis and Walker 1988). These young people are not accustomed to spending long periods of time away from home, and they might be apprehensive about being on their own. Away from the support of their families, they can feel incomplete and lonely (Carnegie Foundation 1989). They might question their ability to make proper decisions on their own. Beginning with the selection of the school and continuing to the selection of a major, the family's influence can be decisive, and it will more likely than not be respected. Depending on the distance from or proximity to traditional values, virtually all of the ethnic and racial minority groups and subgroups have populations to whom this cultural description of family applies. If an institution wants to recruit American Indian students, for example, an awareness of the importance of the family network to those students' well-being must be demonstrated in the recruitment workshops and seminars they will attend. Parents and other family members should be encouraged to participate, accommodated at the seminar, and addressed directly. If possible, they should be greeted in their tribal language. Recruiters should make personal appointments, perhaps at home, with those families who may have concerns not addressed at the seminar.

Normative social structure. In many minority cultures, the social organization is more formal and less flexible than in American society. Prescribed roles within the culture mean that individuals work together to achieve common goals. Unconventional behavior that does not conform to the norms of the group is frowned upon, and social pressure is exerted on those who exhibit behavior that serves individual rather than community goals. Individuals are expected to put aside interests that could conflict with the good of the group, and cooperation is valued highly. These social conventions could result in passive and unobtrusive behavior in group settings (National Coalition 1988). Because this social organization exists in Asian cultures, recruiting Cambodian or Laotian students, for example, should involve individual or one-to-one contact. Recruiters must be willing to supplement the larger group format with private consultations so that students will have an opportunity to express their own interests and apprehensions. Individual contacts could be conducted in a formal manner, consistent with the student's culture.

Group identity. Relationships with others in the community are important in the cultures of minorities. Interpersonal relationships weigh heavily in the individual's cultural experience (Bowler, Rauch, and Schwarzer 1986). The opinions of others who are held in high regard, whether family or friends, matter a great deal, and the importance of belonging to a community and identifying with a set or subset of that community is strong, bringing with it a sense of group bonding. Consequently, loyalty to the group is valued highly, and actions that signal a separation from the group can result in feelings of alienation and misgiving. The group identity may be powerful enough to dissuade the individual from realizing personal objectives that could even be in his or her best interest out of fear of being rejected by the group. Such is the case among many African-American youth who are potential college students. In recruiting these students, the college must therefore be prepared to go a step beyond the standard program and provide services like counseling to help them work through conflicts arising from this cultural dilemma.

Cultural concepts of time. American society is commonly described as oriented toward the future. Intricate planning, delayed rewards, present sacrifice for future gain are concepts typical of American mainstream culture. But these ideas about time do not necessarily exist in other cultures. On the contrary, many minority cultures are much more oriented toward the present (Dupuis and Walker 1988). Concern is focused on meeting immediate needs and solving immediate problems, on living fully in the present and extracting as much as possible from the moment at hand. Because the future cannot be governed, it is addressed when it becomes the present. These ideas about time are manifested in a variety of ways, such as by attending to domestic routines on a daily basis or by organizing and participating in spontaneous, rather than planned, activities. These concepts are directly opposed to many of the organizational and structural requirements at American colleges and universities. For many Hispanic students, whose culture embodies the present time, this discord can create what might be avoidable difficulties. With Hispanic students, recruiters should convey the long-range benefits of college mainly within a context that emphasizes short-term gains. Placing emphasis on what will happen after graduation, four or five years away, will not necessarily motivate Hispanic students to apply to college. Additionally, recruiters should understand that, in many cases, Hispanic students might be interested in college without having planned for it financially, calling for close financial aid and personal counseling during recruitment.

Dependence versus independence. All cultures do not share the mainstream ideal of a self-sufficient, assertive, goal-directed individual. In many minority cultures, an almost contradictory set of values prevails. In the Hispanic culture, for example, relying on others for assistance and support is normal social behavior (Oakland and Ramos-Cancel 1985), in Asian cultures, being reflective or reserved is not considered a sign of weakness but of appropriate conduct, and among

American Indians, promoting cooperative decision making by groups rather than individuals is valued and fostered (Badwound and Tierney 1988; Dupuis and Walker 1988). Yet the presence of one or a combination of these characteristics, especially in minorities, can easily cause them to be categorized as lacking the capacity to be independent. Colleges and universities must recognize that minority students frequently possess other cultural qualities and characteristics that can support them in being successful, despite the fact they might not exhibit the independence valued in American mainstream culture. Their success will depend largely on the university's accommodation of alternative cultural styles.

Facts and figures: A solid foundation

Good planning is based on accurate information. It is important not only to know the facts about minority education in general, but also to understand the situation of minorities at the local institution (Green 1989; National Center 1989). The first element in building a successful recruitment plan therefore is solid institutional research. A careful analysis of data collected by race and ethnicity will accomplish several things. First, it will form the basis for developing various profiles of minority students, indicating who stays, who leaves, when, and under what conditions. These profiles will reveal specific conditions the college needs to know to have a complete picture of minority education at the institution. A side benefit of having this factual information is that it will dispel any prevailing myths about the academic profile of minority students. Second, by providing the statistical foundation, an institutional audit will influence the direction or focus of recruitment. For these data to be useful in terms of understanding the subtleties that could affect specific ethnic minorities, it is essential that the statistical analyses be performed relative to each minority subgroup rather than for the groups as a whole. The disaggregated data will flag information that otherwise would go unnoticed. Finally, performing an institutional audit at the outset of planning for recruitment will serve as a benchmark for evaluating the progress and effectiveness of the plan. Minimally, the data collected according to racial and ethnic subgroup should include the following information:

Overall enrollments. The most basic statistic to institutional research, this information is rarely collected separately for the

... it is essential that the statistical analyses be performed relative to each minority subgroup rather than for the groups as a whole.

various subgroups within the major minority categories. Disaggregated data will indicate the proportion of minority students at the institution within each subgroup and the trends in their patterns of enrollment. Reviewed periodically, these data will reveal low enrollments of a particular subgroup and the fluctuations that might occur within each group as a result of migration and demographic changes.

Retention rates by semester. It is fundamental to a good recruitment plan to know whether or not minority students exhibit a higher dropout rate than nonminorities and the degree to which it might affect each subgroup. Analyzing persistence by semester for each ethnic subgroup will reveal patterns specific to the institution. Correlated with other factors, this information will aid in developing timely interventions.

Graduation rates. The complete picture of minority education cannot be fully understood unless the rate of graduation is known, but it is also important to determine the length of time needed to complete a degree. Consequently, rates beyond the traditional two-year and four-year exit points should be tracked.

Transfer rates. The objective of determining transfer rates is to determine the effectiveness of articulation between two-year and four-year programs. Senior colleges should therefore look at the number of minority students who transfer into the college, the point in their academic careers at which they do so, and the two-year schools from which they come. Two-year colleges need to establish the number of students who transfer to four-year programs, regardless of whether they have completed the associate degree.

Academic performance by semester. Because GPA has been shown to affect retention and graduation rates, this information should be collected early and reviewed frequently. Understanding the academic profile of each minority subgroup will help determine whether or not recruitment strategies combined with interventions such as academic support programs are indicated. In addition, correlating academic performance and high school origin will indicate the relative academic preparation of students from various feeder schools.

Enrollments by curriculum. Research indicates that, depending on their ethnicity, minority students cluster around certain curricula and underenroll in others. For example, the literature clearly shows that curricula in science and technology attract very few African-Americans, Hispanics, and American Indians. In fact, enrollments among these students in the sciences, mathematics, and engineering are so low that some researchers consider this fact to signal a national crisis, given the changing demography of the country. For Asian-Americans the problem is the converse: High numbers of Asian students enroll in science and technology, while few enroll in the social sciences.

Identifying minority enrollment rates in each curriculum will determine the degree to which this phenomenon occurs locally. An institution can design interventions and direct recruitment efforts to help counterbalance these trends, although it should be recognized that this issue cannot be addressed through recruitment alone.

An integrated design: Linking objectives
Another principal characteristic of an effective recruitment plan is that it be constructed from an institutionwide perspective (Pulliams 1988). Because recruitment is a starting point and not an end objective in minority education, it should be integrated with other institutional goals (Christoffel 1986). Involvement in both the academic and the social aspects of college life are important determinants in the success of minority students in higher education (Langer 1987; Mallinckrodt and Sedlecek 1987; Nora 1987; Tinto 1987). Architects of the recruitment plan must recognize that such factors as social integration, academic performance, retention, and campus pluralism are closely related to recruitment. Research conducted in these areas will provide the basis from which to establish these connections.

Factors that surface in the institutional audit, such as low graduation rates, could indicate problem areas for minority students that cannot be resolved through recruitment as an isolated function. This information is nonetheless valuable to recruitment, because it will place the institution in a better position to integrate recruitment with other institutional initiatives related to minority education. For example, if the low graduation rates of Vietnamese students were determined to be a result of limited proficiency in English, a strategy could be designed that simultaneously addresses the academic preparation of potential Vietnamese students, such as a high school/college collaborative program focusing on instruction in language. Such an initiative would ensure that the students the institution is recruiting are academically prepared to succeed and ultimately to graduate.

Relative to social integration, an institution might determine through research that African-American students who are actively involved in clubs or other organizations fare better than those who are not. By using this information in recruitment, the institution can accomplish two goals: to devise a strategy for recruitment specifically related to these findings and to address the retention of newly enrolled African-American students through better social integration. This goal might be accomplished, for example, by reviewing the application and general intake forms of African-American students to identify their special interests, perhaps playing a musical instrument, working on the school paper, or participating in student government. A system could then be devised to match these students' interests with existing clubs and organizations on campus and to arrange personal contact through these offices with these potential students. With a holistic, multifaceted approach, this strategy combines both the recruitment and retention of African-American students through social integration.

Ethnic studies centers, departments, or programs on campus have been recognized in the literature as important elements in the education of minorities. A college might determine from its own institutional research, for example, that American Indian students who regularly attend programs and participate in activities at the Native American center on campus are better able to negotiate the university system and to establish stronger social networks with other American Indians. To capitalize on one of the institution's identified strengths, the Native American center should be fully integrated in the college's recruitment plan, perhaps by engaging the faculty and staff of the center in recruitment. Ideal role models, these individuals can relate to the American Indian community the center's programs and activities by addressing small groups at local schools, visiting potential students at home, and telephoning prospective students. By combining recruitment with the people and activities of an ethnic studies center, this strategy addresses social integration on campus and the "comfort factor," two variables in the persistence of minority students.

Specificity: The key to a measurable plan

When working toward an objective they believe in, most people want to know whether or not their efforts are carrying them toward their goal and, if not, why not. No one wants to invest time, money, and energy in something that yields no results. Strong evaluation is therefore an essential component of the recruitment plan (Middleton and Mason 1987). As an institutional investment, recruitment is accountable to the college community, and it will be necessary to report on its effectiveness. Faculty, staff, administrators, students—all those who participate in the process—have a stake in its success and are entitled to be kept informed about its performance, whether positive or, on occasion, negative. It is even more important if the project is controversial at the institution. In that case, the frequent reporting of objective facts and figures will help counteract misconceptions.

At the same time, those responsible for recruitment will want to determine whether the human and financial resources invested are being expended efficiently. In an era of shrinking budgets and difficult fiscal decisions, a project of this nature could be vulnerable. In addition to assessing programmatic initiatives, therefore, the financial aspect of the project should be part of the evaluation, because clear and convincing evidence that resources are used resourcefully and responsibly will strengthen the project.

Complete and accurate information concerning the outcomes of the plan for recruitment will require continuous monitoring. Especially fruitful methods should be identified so they can be further developed, while ineffective ones must be assessed and reconsidered. And it will be easier to accomplish if the goals and objectives of the plan are stated in specific, measurable terms. A plan for recruitment whose goals are too broad and undefined can result in limiting rather than promoting recruitment, because outcomes will be difficult or impossible to measure. Vague and open-ended objectives will not indicate whether results are all they could be.

A general and vaguely stated objective, such as "to increase the enrollment of Hispanic students," leaves too much room for unanswered questions. The desired outcome remains ambiguous, inviting subjective assessments of success. For example, what would prevent a favorable evaluation of this objective even if only three new Hispanic students were enrolled? Or suppose all the new recruits were middle-class Hispanic students from a foreign country or male; would the objective have been met? No one of these outcomes per se is unacceptable; the point is to ensure that the result achieved is the one that was planned for. Stating objectives specifically will force the plan's architects to think each objective through and to articulate it in concrete terms. In this way, the desired outcome will be clear and measurable.

For example, a more detailed plan might explicitly state this objective as follows:

To increase Hispanic enrollment by 5 percent (approximately 50 students). Of this 5 percent:
• At least 40 percent will be female;
• At least six students will be Puerto Ricans from U.S. urban areas;
• At least six students will be Puerto Ricans residing in Puerto Rico;
• At least 15 students will be Chicanos from the Chicago area.
The remaining number will be randomly recruited.

Depending on the institution's needs, it is important when defining objectives for recruitment to be specific not only about who will be recruited but also about how it should be approached. In another example, a generally stated objective like "to increase the number of American Indian transfer students" might be made more specifically:

To increase Navajo transfer enrollments by 50 percent (approximately 30 students). Of this number:
• Five students will be from tribal colleges;
• Six students will be recruited through the Native American studies center;
• Six students will be recruited through a new joint admissions program with an area community college;
• Thirteen students will be recruited through the existing proactive transfer program with an area community college.
At least 20 percent of all students will be recruited into science curricula.

Of course, objectives at this level will not be complete until an accompanying set of activities is developed. In the previous objective to recruit Navajo students, each strategy defined should specify how it will be accomplished and by whom. The strategy using the Native American studies center, for example, might be written as follows:

- Six students will be recruited through the Native American studies center and:
  - Counselors will make weekly home visits;
  - Native American faculty will conduct small-group sessions at targeted community colleges;
  - The Dean of Science and Technology will host a group of Navajo community college students visiting the Native American studies center;
  - Brochures and open invitations to visit the Native American studies center will be mailed;
  - Native American upperclassmen will follow up with phone calls after the mailing.

Defining specific objectives of the recruitment plan will make it necessary for those involved to think through proposed ideas and to express them precisely. The more concrete and specific the terms of the plan, the better able the institution will be to evaluate it, attributing success to the elements that are effective and identifying strategies that do not produce results. Periodic evaluations will provide the data needed to communicate the plan's progress to the college community, an essential component of any institutionwide initiative.

A holistic approach: The team

A holistic approach to recruitment incorporates a variety of constituencies, bringing together representatives of each— from the initial development of the recruitment plan to the implementation of specific strategies for recruitment (Pulliams 1988; Tysinger and Whiteside 1987). Three principal constituencies are administrators, faculty, and counselors and professional staff.

Administrators. Ideally, the initiative of collegewide recruitment should be organized at the presidential or near-presidential level (Rivera 1986; Wilson 1986). Leadership at these levels will signal to the college community that creating diversity on campus is a priority and that the administration is committed to accomplishing the goal. Moreover, individuals from the institution's various constituencies will generally be more likely to participate and cooperate if the initiative comes from the top. Even if organized at some other level, however, it remains important to have the president's or another top administrator's endorsement, because doing so naturally lends authority to the project.

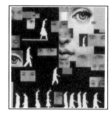

Because a strong effort in recruiting minority students necessitates evaluating present policies and possibly creating new ones, the participation of top-level administrators is fundamental. Many of the main responsibilities of high-level administrators include developing, implementing, and monitoring policy. Depending on the issue, policy might be developed elsewhere in the institution but implemented and monitored by the administration, such as with the case of curriculum.

Considered an academic concern, policy related to the curriculum falls within the purview of the faculty, but it is the administration's responsibility to implement it. On other matters and depending on the institution, consultation with other constituencies could be necessary or well advised to formulate policy, but the final decisions rest with the administration. An example might be procedures for student appeals. Regardless of whether administrators are directly or indirectly responsible for the institution's policies regarding recruitment of minority students, they are central to the discussion. Once a plan for recruitment is operational, the administrators will monitor whether the outcomes of the plan satisfy institutional policies.

Because a collegewide, uninvested perspective is needed to pull a team together to work on recruitment, a primary responsibility of administrators is to recruit and appoint its members. Much of the success of the entire effort will depend on the individuals involved. Consequently, the people responsible for the effort should be respected and held in high regard by their peers; faculty must be tenured, full-time faculty with senior rank. Providing broad representation from all sectors of the institution, including student affairs, academic affairs, and special programs, should also be considered. The team must include a full range of people, from those working in front-line positions to those in the upper administrative ranks. Attention should also be paid to ensuring representation from various races and ethnicities. With their bird's-eye view of the college and their ability to identify individuals with influence from each area, administrators are in the best position to see that these criteria are met.

In an ideal world, instituting change on campus would be simple to accomplish and would require no additional resources. Realistically, however, any significant effort, such as improving the campus climate and increasing the number of minority students, will almost certainly require resources. Among other things, they may include additional secretarial support, release time for faculty, or more professional staff. Because allocating resources is an administrative responsibility, it requires the support of administrators in positions of authority and influence regarding the institution's budget. Indeed, without committing dollars to this initiative, it is unlikely to yield significant results.

It is the administration's responsibility to communicate with the college community about the purpose, goals, progress, and evaluation of minority recruitment, which will require developing a system of communication in concert with the other constituencies of the project and devising the methods and techniques to disseminate the information to the college as a whole. By reporting on the status of the project at meetings—cabinet, faculty senate, institutional planning, and student government—administrators can ensure that all segments of the college community remain informed and have the opportunity to exchange views.

Faculty. Faculty are essential constituents in recruitment for many reasons. First, in the design of the plan for recruitment, policy issues like standards might need to be decided, and faculty are critical in this discussion. And for recruitment to be recognized as an academic as well as an administrative matter, faculty must be involved, because they are the natural advocates for such a position and they are the natural conduits through which it can be enacted. While all faculty, of course, will not be directly involved in the design and implementation of the institution's plan for recruitment, they could be kept informed through their representatives at governing bodies like the faculty senate. Indeed, by placing the subject of recruiting minority students on the agenda of the faculty senate, it will be recognized as a central rather than a marginal matter.

Second, because a greater minority presence on campus signifies change, the active and informed participation of such a principal constituency as the faculty is essential for success, especially when the change concerns the student body, with which faculty are so intricately involved. Professors have the most direct and constant contact with students after they enroll. They know students' academic needs, they design curriculum, and they evaluate performance. It is therefore natural they should be in the forefront of the effort to bring new students to campus. As the complexion of the student body changes, faculty should be prepared through an awareness of how the changes were planned for, and they should understand the cultural diversity of each subgroup.

Third, in addition to the important contributions they can make in designing the institution's plan to recruit minority students, faculty are specially qualified to implement certain strategies for recruitment. Through their general knowledge of the institution, its requirements and standards, and the intricacies of the system, faculty are in an excellent position to convey important information to students and parents. More important than all of this, however, is the intellectual excitement many faculty possess for their field. Professors who have a love for their discipline and can transmit that enthusiasm to young and impressionable minds can be the most effective recruiters.

Counselors and professional staff. In a traditional model, it is admissions counselors and recruiters who are mainly responsible for identifying, locating, and recruiting students to the campus. While in many colleges this approach has met with some success in increasing the enrollment of minority students, it has a narrow range of participants and as a result might not realize the institution's full potential for recruiting minorities. Professionals in other areas of the institution who have experience working with minority students have much to offer the initiative. Such individuals often have a special commitment to minority students, a knowledge of minority communities, and an understanding of their various cultures. In this category, therefore, key personnel include admissions counselors, recruiters, and the professional staff of minority offices and special programs.

Decades of front-line experience make this constituency's contribution significant not only in implementing recruitment but also during design, when the scope and method of the plan for recruitment are being developed. With their wealth of knowledge and expertise concerning recruitment and minority communities, the perspective of experienced counselors and professional staff can inform the discussion and keep it within the practical realm. Armed with good intentions but a lack of experience specific to recruitment, administrators and faculty might propose unrealistic objectives or initiatives that are not feasible to implement. The participation of counselors and professional staff in the design of the plan for recruitment will balance the discussion.

Counselors and professional staff will execute much of the day-to-day implementation of strategies for recruitment. They will therefore be in the best position to monitor the pulse of the plan and determine its progress. This important work, which might be accomplished through the systematic collection of objective and subjective data, detailed record keeping, and regular reporting, is critical to evaluating progress and modifying future plans. Counselors and professional staff therefore play a vital role in developing systems and organizing the operations relative to evaluation.

This aspect of the role of counselors necessarily calls for yet another dimension of their participation—the timely and thorough reporting to other members of the team regarding the status of the plan. In any collaborative effort, the regular sharing of information among the parties greatly enhances its effectiveness and is fundamental to maintaining cohesion in the project. By communicating regularly, everyone involved will be able to identify problem areas and will be in a better position to offer modifications or solutions.

Models of organization. Members of the recruitment team or committee could be organized in several different ways. The committee could be an institutionwide body organized at the top, reporting directly to the president or another top administrator and transmitting the committee's decisions and recommendations downward through the various committee members themselves and their constituents. In a second model, the collegewide committee would be organized at the midmanagement level, most likely in the recruitment or admissions office, and would probably report to the director of that office. The committee's decisions and recommendations would be transmitted both horizontally and vertically through the recruitment team. Although organized at this level, this model can also be effective if it has strong and committed leadership, most often emanating from the chair. Both models, however, need the endorsement of top administrators to gain the authority necessary to create institutional change.

Implementation

An effective, holistic plan for recruitment implies the participation of a broad spectrum of individuals at the college or university, an approach that applies not only in designing the plan but also in implementing it. Individuals representing different segments of the college community—including administrators, faculty, and professional staff—have diverse responsibilities and expertise that are essential if the plan is to be well executed and successful. By capitalizing on all the talents of individuals at its disposal, the institution can create an efficient and cost-effective program to recruit minorities.

A strategy will be more effective with a specific minority group or subgroup if the particular cultural characteristics of that group are considered. The following strategies include examples of the kinds of activities suitable to one or another of the three constituencies described in the previous subsection. To some extent, however, the assignment of a given strategy to a particular category is flexible. Several of these activities require the cooperation and participation of a cross section of individuals from different areas of the institution or even from outside. Many factors can affect the way in which the strategies might or might not apply to different colleges or universities. Institutional characteristics, such as sector, size, traditions, and protocol, will affect potential adaptations of any type of strategy and will determine the locus of responsibility for implementing it.

Strategies for administrators

Alternative admissions. Traditionally, colleges and universities use high school grades, achievement test scores, class rank, and recommendations as predictors of academic success for determining acceptance. With nontraditional measures, such as *alternative admissions,* the weighting of these criteria is different (Berger 1988a; Fincher 1975; Martinez-Perez 1978). For example, because some minority groups have been shown to perform less successfully on standardized achievement tests (Ascher 1983; Astin et al. 1982; Navarro 1985; Payan et al. 1984), this criterion would not be considered as heavily, while others, such as letters of recommendation, would be given more weight (Wright 1978). For example, the University of Massachusetts–Boston has found that SAT scores are not predictors of GPA and therefore admits students based on nontraditional measures.

When an evaluation based on normal criteria would have precluded admission, a *portfolio,* originally used more frequently in the creative and performing arts, would override all other criteria. Special writing ability, for example, would be recognized. Ramapo State College in New Jersey has provided this opportunity for minority students for more than 15 years.

Higher education institutions use *contracts* to motivate minority students to aspire to college by guaranteeing admission while they are still in high school, provided they meet the criteria specified in the contract. It does not mean that admission standards are lowered; rather, the student no longer has to compete for the seat. Cornell University in New York, for example, contracts with American Indian students in local high schools for admission to the university.

Higher education institutions use contracts to motivage minority students to aspire to college. . . .

Transfer programs. Because so many minority students attend two-year colleges, these schools have become a resource for recruiting minority students into four-year institutions (Illinois Community College Board 1986; Samuels 1985). Although these programs are not new, they did not always address the difficulties inherent in earning a four-year degree from two different institutions (Guichard and Cepeda 1986), and transfer students would sometimes find it necessary to study for a semester or more at the senior college before achieving third-year status.

Through interinstitutional cooperation, the course offerings in two-year and four-year degree programs are articulated so that students who have earned an associate degree in a specific major can enter the senior college degree program at the third-year level. To encourage and facilitate the recruitment of minority students into senior colleges, *joint admissions* programs ease the transition for students who successfully complete the associate degree by indicating acceptance to the four-year college at the time the student enters the community college program. La Guardia Community College and Queens College, for example, both part of CUNY, have established an effective joint admissions program through which community college students transfer to baccalaureate programs.

The goal of a *proactive transfer* program is to identify minority students who are potential transfers to a four-year program at an early stage in their college careers. Acceptance into such a program guarantees acceptance into the four-year institution. In this model, the liaison from the community college recruits students into the transfer program. Meeting regularly with the liaison from the four-year institution, they design workshops, seminars, and activities that bring the students to the senior college campus. Students who complete the program and transfer have the advantage of having had sustained contact with the senior-college liaison, who becomes their counselor or adviser during the first semester. Glassboro State College in New Jersey, for example, conducts Project PROMIST, a proactive transfer program that fosters close collaboration between Glassboro and its surrounding community colleges to increase the number of minority student transfers.

Scholarships/financial assistance. One of the most essential ingredients in a plan to recruit minority students is comprehensive financial aid (Hanford 1982; Samuels 1985). Because so many minority students have no other means of financing a college education, providing financial aid is critical. Most full scholarships and complete financial assistance programs are based on merit and limited to the best and the brightest. Just as using alternative admissions criteria is necessary to break the barrier of access for large numbers of minority students, alternative criteria for awarding scholarships, grants, and other financial aid are also important (Committee on Education 1985; South Carolina Commission 1987). For example, the University of Colorado provides reduced tuition for American Indians enrolling in the university's programs.

Colleges and private industries have devised creative ways to underwrite the costs of higher education. One company provides full financial backing for a minority student the college identifies as having potential in the specific discipline of interest to the sponsor.

Athletics-related recruiting. Athletics has long been an avenue by which a few talented minority students have had access to larger, more competitive universities. Through special scholarships, alternative admissions, and aggressive recruiting, such students reach campuses armed with a variety of academic backgrounds. In the minority community, however, athletics-related recruiting has become an item of concern. The academic needs of students recruited for their athletic prowess are often only minimally satisfied or neglected (Lapchick 1989).

As a strategy for recruitment, athletics-related recruiting can be effective for the institution and a valuable opportunity for the student. A large percentage of minority students with above-average though not exceptional abilities in sports do not consider college because of academic or socioeconomic reasons. Conversely, institutions have not fully exploited the motivating power that sports can engender. With the proper guidance and support, this pool of minority youth can become another source of successful students.

Four plus One. The idea behind this strategy is to address the underrepresentation of minorities at both the undergraduate and graduate levels simultaneously. A university offering both degrees would recruit a student into the graduate program at the beginning of his or her college career rather than at the end. In Four plus One programs, students receive dual acceptances and are awarded the fifth year—the master's degree program—free. At first glance, this creative idea appears to focus on recruitment into graduate school. Guaranteed acceptance into and financial support for graduate school, however, are attractive ways to build undergraduate enrollments, particularly in undersubscribed curricula.

The potential for this program is great. For the cost of one year of graduate study, undergraduate enrollments are increased, graduate enrollments are increased, and the pool of potential Ph.D. candidates is expanded. The University of Rochester in New York offers a Fifth Year Free program to attract minority undergraduate students to the university.

Strategies for faculty
Joint ventures. Collaboration between colleges and other entities, such as schools, community-based organizations, and businesses, has become more popular in recent years. These joint ventures share resources, avoid duplication, stimulate innovation, and increase the effectiveness of the cooperating institutions with regard to the education of minorities. Collaboration is effective not only in terms of cost, however; it

can also improve the efficiency and effectiveness of each separate partner. New structures and streamlined procedures can result, without compromising each individual partner's distinct identity (Lynton 1981). The best reflect an awareness on the part of the higher education community of the interrelatedness of the objectives of recruitment, retention, and graduation.

Higher education institutions have exerted their greatest efforts toward the participation of minorities by developing and operating special *school/college collaborative programs.* Of course, the availability of outside funding from the state and federal governments, private foundations, and business and industry has played a large part in fostering their development, but institutions have created an enormous variety of approaches and activities to carry out their goals (Galligani 1984; Kimmel, Martino, and Tomkins 1988; Wilbur et al. 1988). These programs encompass all facets of educating minorities, from early intervention in elementary school to supporting gifted and talented high school students.

A frequently used model focuses on improving academic preparation by emphasizing the development of basic skills, cognitive and study skills, and knowledge in specific content areas (Jordan 1981; Mendoza 1988). Two important types of models are used. In one, the college has a presence in the school through faculty members and staff who visit the school to give seminars, teach, and participate in developing curricula. The other type brings students to the college campus for instruction or special activities (Halcon 1988). In cases where students live some distance from the college, the program is conducted as a summer residency program. The target population as well as the goals and objectives of programs in this model vary. Some provide remedial instruction, while others concentrate on academic enrichment. Given the scarcity of resources in many school districts, collaborative programs provide school students an opportunity to use laboratories and state-of-the-art equipment that would otherwise be unavailable to them. The College of Staten Island and several other units of CUNY, for example, provide academic instruction and support for science, engineering, and computer science students in a partnership between schools and colleges called the Science and Technology Entry Program (STEP) funded by the New York Department of Education.

Besides academic-based activities, collaborative programs also foster personal development. Through workshops with teachers and other professionals like psychologists and counselors, students explore themselves as individuals and as members of society by clarifying values, developing the ability to lead, and engaging in interpersonal communication (National Puerto Rican Coalition 1989). For example, ASPIRA, a national, Puerto Rican, community-based organization, works with high schools and colleges to help develop the potential for leadership among high school students.

Because the regular school curriculum is limited in offering the history and culture of minority children, collaborative programs have been developed to fill this void. Co-sponsored activities, perhaps focusing on Puerto Rican Heritage Month and Black History Month and celebrating the cultural backgrounds and traditions of people of color, teach the students to value and take pride in their heritage. Faculty and administrators at Mount Saint Mary's College in Los Angeles, for example, have developed strategies to use cultural differences as a positive part of the educational process to teach students more effectively.

In recognition that the education of minority children is affected by the social and economic circumstances of their lives, a holistic model addressing all aspects simultaneously has been developed that provides academic support and personal and cultural enrichment through the *school,* the *college,* and *community-based organizations.* These partnerships help meet family needs, such as housing, food, counseling, and health care. Professionals from each of the three components communicate with each other, working together as a team to resolve the problems. New York state has over 50 Liberty Partnership programs, which require the inclusion of a community-based organization in collaboration with schools and colleges to provide at-risk junior high and high school students with academic and family support services.

Private businesses and industries have become increasingly involved with colleges in the education of minorities, providing grants, in-kind services, and training and internship opportunities (National Action Council 1988). Activities focusing on career development, in which high school students explore and experience the world of work, take place either at the college campus or on site. Studying in seminars and workshops with minority role models as guest speakers, students learn about the kinds of career opportunities available and the academic programs necessary to pursue them (Halcon 1988).

Because businesses are interested in developing the academic skills of their workers (Berger 1988a), collaboratives have been developed in which employees, sponsored by their employers, enroll in college to begin or complete a degree, leading to an improved status or promotion. This type of collaborative program among *colleges, business, and industry* is a potential resource for institutions of higher education interested in recruiting adult minority students. AT&T, for example, brings high school students to company sites, where college faculty and company staff conduct workshops; it also provides summer internships.

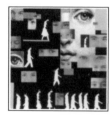

Addressing student groups. Whether faculty go to the local schools to address students or meet with them on campus, the benefits of having direct faculty-student contact are many. When faculty members can transmit the enthusiasm they feel for their discipline, it can be a powerful stimulus, especially for minority students, who in fact might never have met a college professor before. In many instances, students might have only a vague notion of what a given discipline encompasses or, in practical terms, what studying in that discipline entails. These forums provide an opportunity for minority students to explore various academic areas of study with an expert in the field. To make students feel comfortable enough to ask questions and participate openly, these groups should be small and informal.

Classroom and laboratory audits. No substitute exists for first-hand experience. For students to begin to understand what college would be like, a personal visit to a college class or seminar can be one of the most effective methods. Most minority students are the first in their families to consider a college education. Consequently, they have not had the benefit of family discussions about college life or trips to college campuses. Permitting potential students to sit in on their classes and taking a few moments to discuss the student's impressions afterward create an opportunity that only the faculty can offer. In doing so, they provide a special occasion for students to gain a personal perspective on the way college classes are conducted and on what might be expected of them in such a situation.

Role models among minority faculty. Too often minority faculty are asked to be personally involved in all minority-related issues at the college or university. Not only is this role taxing on the individual, but numerous extracurricular demands can also seriously detract from the time and effort they would normally need to devote to their own scholarly and professional efforts. Other strategies mentioned in this section apply to both majority and minority faculty, but in this case, the involvement of minority faculty is key.

Because most minority students have had limited exposure to minority adults in prestigious or otherwise successful positions of authority, personal interactions with minority faculty members can make a lasting impression. Many minority faculty have had to overcome obstacles similar to those faced by today's students. In sharing their personal experiences and points of view about setting and reaching their own goals in life, these individuals can inspire minority students to focus on their own aspirations. Because of their unique vantage point, minority faculty can provide valuable guidance and advice that others cannot.

Strategies for counselors
Public relations and information. The classic strategy of recruitment by disseminating information about the institution has been adapted to reach more minority constituencies by creating information centers in urban areas and minority communities. They include providing advice and guidance regarding postsecondary alternatives by experienced counselors and advisers. Often the information is provided in languages other than English, and technical assistance in filling out college applications, financial aid forms, and other documents is provided.

Because the cost of operating these centers can be prohibitive for a single institution, consortia are developed, with the additional benefit of providing guidance and direction regarding choices of postsecondary educational opportunities.

To reach prospective students in communities where languages other than English predominate, *media using native languages* (newspaper ads, television and radio commercials) are common and useful means of spreading information about college programs and services. Hostos Community College, part of CUNY in the Bronx, for example, advertises in the Spanish media, targeting information in particular to women returning to college.

Direct mail and follow-up phoning have been tailored to provide a more personal focus in the recruitment of minority students. In this strategy, the literature that describes the college reflects the ethnicity of students and highlights the special programs and activities available for that particular group. After the mailings are sent, special staff or student recruiters of the student's same ethnic background call them to answer questions and encourage them to visit the campus. The University of Texas at Austin, for example, in its SHARE program (Students Helping Admissions in the Recruitment Effort), employs student aides who phone minority students who have applied to the university as well as students whose names are located through the PSAT search as competitors in the National Merit and National Achievement Scholarship programs.

Campus visits. For colleges to be more competitive in an already competitive market, some selective institutions that recruit students nationally have expanded the concept of "college days" to a full weekend orientation, all expenses paid. For many of the students, experiencing the atmosphere of the college first hand would not have been possible otherwise.

This model can be adapted to target the large portion of minority students who are not part of the top 10 percent and who are unable for financial reasons to visit college campuses they are considering. These students frequently choose an institution based on limited knowledge gleaned from the literature or information they receive from friends. Naturally, a positive experience is likely to result in a successful recruitment for the college. For example, Brown University in Rhode Island, Dartmouth in New Hampshire, and Wesleyan in Connecticut pay air fare and other expenses for minority students' visits to campus.

Parental involvement. Some strategies developed for general recruitment and adapted for recruiting minority students have met with less success than expected. Parents' involvement has always been an important and useful recruitment tool, but if it is to function effectively in recruiting minorities, it will have to be tailored to suit their needs. The involvement of Hispanic parents should occur, for example, when their children are still in elementary school, because by high school in some cities, more than 50 percent of the Hispanic student population has already dropped out (Fernandez 1989). Another limitation of programs to involve parents is that too often the focus is on middle-class minority parents, ignoring the large percentage of parents with limited education and financial means (Wilson 1986).

Cultural factors and family values play a significant part in the decisions minority students make regarding higher education. In cases where residency is involved, protective attitudes, especially toward women, can have a decisive influence on the student's ultimate choice. Personal and sustained contact, when necessary in the family's native language, is one way to foster understanding, build trust, and allay the family's fears (Ramon 1985; Woodland and Goldstein 1984).

Successful recruiters of minority students have indicated the importance of maintaining a presence in the community. They can do so by attending local churches and cultural and civic activities, and by working with community-based organizations. Creative initiatives have combined recruitment with social functions that the college sponsors for the benefit of the community.

Successful recruiters of minority students have indicated the importance of maintaining a presence in the community.

It is equally important for parents and family to experience campus life. Strategies organized around this purpose may focus on one-time activities, such as festivals or celebrations honoring minority cultures, or a talk given by an individual recognized in the community. Other strategies of this type include the development of ongoing programs (Commission on California 1985) involving both the student and the family in extended activities, such as instruction in a second language and basic skills. Programs of this type have a dual benefit: Besides the obvious contribution to the parents' personal development, the experience of participating in college activities increases parents' understanding of college life and helps them to better support their children at home. Arizona State University, for example, targets young Hispanic female students and their mothers by providing them with educational experiences on the university campus.

Liaisons as recruiters. In minority groups like American Indians, students are more likely to respond to encouragement to go to college when that encouragement is provided by another American Indian (Kleinfeld, Cooper, and Kyle 1987). An interesting and innovative strategy for recruitment was developed in the Yukon-Koyukuk high school district in Alaska. The postsecondary counselor program, based at the high schools, recruits potential American Indian college students for a variety of colleges in the area. The key element in this attractive program is the high school counselor, who continues to counsel and advise the student and family, not only to the point of enrolling in college, but also through his or her entire undergraduate career. The long-term, personal relationship established with a counselor from the student's home town and high school offers significant support, affecting both college recruitment and persistence.

Colleges are now hiring "student ambassadors" to help in the recruitment of new minority students. This practice is based on the concept that prospective students will naturally be more inclined to listen with care to students who share the experiences they have had at a college.

Other individuals, such as high school teachers, are also employed in recruitment. Their direct and sustained contact with students whom the college is interested in enables teachers to assist students in determining what college to attend. Teacher liaisons can also play an important role in influencing students who might not be considering college as an option. Valencia Community College in Florida, for example, works with high school teachers in the surrounding community to help identify students and facilitate their enrollment in college.

Recruiting through social activities. A problem recruiters often face at many of their functions is a low turnout of minority students. One way to address this problem is by holding activities in the local minority communities, rather than at the college, and combining them with social activities. In this way, people who would not ordinarily attend a college recruitment session may do so because of the social attraction. For example, a recruitment session might be scheduled between 7:00 and 8:00 P.M. at a local church and then followed by a dance featuring a familiar music group. While many young people might be attracted by the anticipation of socializing

at the dance, those who attend will have the benefit of exposure they probably would not have received otherwise. To
ensure participation in the function, organizers could charge
admission to the dance and then waive it for people who
attend the recruitment session. Even for those who choose
to pay the admission, it is good public relations for the college
to host an activity in the minority community, and the investment could pay off at a later date.

SUMMARY, CONCLUSIONS, AND RECOMMENDATIONS FOR FURTHER RESEARCH

Summary and Conclusions

Clearly, improving educational opportunities for ethnic and racial minorities must become more than an objective of the admissions office. It must become an institutional priority.

More and more elementary and high school students come from minority backgrounds, and, according to demographers, their numbers continue to increase dramatically. Yet the proportion of these students who graduate from college is distressingly small.

Such trends cast a shadow over the future of higher education—indeed, over the future of the country. Solutions must be found.

Recruiting more minority students to colleges and universities is certainly one solution. But because the issue involves complicated social, economic, and educational factors, recruitment of minority students is most effective when it also recognizes the other factors that affect the educational success and persistence of minority students.

Higher education institutions have adopted various prescriptive measures to recruit minority students and improve their chances for success, but these measures are infrequently interwoven in an overall, collegewide plan. Incorporating recruitment in other college initiatives, aside from being an efficient use of college resources, also maximizes the college's ability to attract, retain, and graduate more minority students.

Broadening recruitment in this way, however, is more likely to be achieved if the college community recognizes and understands the goals of increasing the presence of people of color and of fostering the values of pluralism and diversity in campus life, and adopts them as an institutional priority. Change of this nature and scope, however, requires commitment, cooperation, and leadership. The literature clearly indicates that institutions are transformed through presidential leadership and expressed institutional commitment.

Such leadership and commitment do not come easily. If the process of recruiting minority students is to have integrity and if institutions are serious about their commitment to minority youth, then recruitment will be a reflective and considered process. To be most effective, it should begin with introspection. What is it about the institution itself that has contributed to the present situation of minorities' low enrollment? Another equally important subject that is integral to

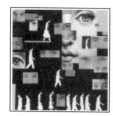

the issue of enrollment is the question of success. If minorities are being enrolled in significant numbers only to drop out after the first or second term, then all the recruitment programs in the world will not serve to achieve the real goals—academic success and graduation.

The problem of minorities' low participation and graduation rates at college is explained to a great extent by a breakdown in the flow of minority students along the educational continuum. While different minority communities can be affected to varying degrees, on the whole, people of color experience much less success than white students. Although the problem of a "leaky educational pipeline" has been discussed in the literature for almost a decade, for Hispanics, African-Americans, American Indians, and many Asian-Americans, the problem in many ways is worse now than before. Colleges and universities need to take an active role in preparing minority youth for the challenges of higher education. Higher education institutions, by cooperating with elementary and secondary schools, parents, business, industry, and government, can provide essential direction and support.

Presidential leadership is needed to provide the inspiration for change and make the recruitment of people of color a central priority at the college. Whether it be to expand the curriculum, offer a broader program of social and cultural activities on campus, or promote racial diversity by enrolling more minority students, the support and courage of all a university's constituencies are necessary. To attain a significant increase in the number of minority students on campus, a strong institutional commitment must be made to forging the kinds of changes required. Without the vision and leadership of the president and other top administrators, the issue is likely to remain marginal.

Focusing on the characteristics of students that affect educational attainment, such as academic preparation and socioeconomic status, will not necessarily guarantee greater success for minority students. Also important are changes in the climate of higher education institutions. College campuses enriched by diversity and embracing a philosophy of cultural pluralism will do much to enhance the participation and success of students from ethnic and racial backgrounds. Colleges and universities that recognize and respond to the demand for greater cultural diversity in the academy will broaden the range of experience for all students.

To be most effective, the plan for recruitment should emerge from an institutional plan. The objectives of the college's plan, however, should be considered as only part of the broader goal of educating and graduating more minority students. Institutions should take a holistic approach to recruitment, integrating recruitment with other educational objectives, such as academic performance, social integration, pluralism, and diversity. In developing and implementing the plan for recruitment, the perspectives of various college constituencies should be considered, as everyone at the college—faculty, administrators, counselors, and professional staff—has an interest and an investment in the ultimate success of all students.

An awareness of cultural differences is an essential part of designing a good plan for recruitment as well as of implementing it. While some strategies for recruitment can be used to recruit students from various ethnic and racial backgrounds, the manner in which the strategies are put into practice and the people involved should depend on who the targeted students are. An awareness of differing cultural values and needs is an essential first step to a truly culturally diverse college campus.

Recommendations for Further Research

The literature concerning the recruitment of minority students would benefit enormously from additional research and development in several important areas. The following ones are the most pressing.

1. Collection, analysis, and interpretation of higher education data concerning minority subpopulations, reported in disaggregated form;
2. Evaluation of model programs to improve the institutional climate and cultural pluralism on college campuses;
3. Evaluation of the various state policies addressing transfer from two-year to four-year colleges;
4. Evaluation of college-based programs designed to increase the rate of minority students' transferring to four-year colleges;
5. Analysis of cultural differences among minority groups and subgroups and their effect on minorities' access and success;
6. Effects of financial aid on minorities' entering college according to ethnic and racial subgroup;

7. Evaluation of collegewide recruitment programs, especially those relating to specific minority groups;
8. Evaluation of innovative strategies for recruitment that are culturally specific;
9. Investigation of factors affecting minority students' success that are other than academic;
10. Evaluation of precollege recruitment programs that emphasize preparation for mathematics and science.

REFERENCES

The Educational Resources Information Center (ERIC) Clearinghouse on Higher Education abstracts and indexes the current literature on higher education for inclusion in ERIC's data base and announcement in ERIC's monthly bibliographic journal, *Resources in Education* (RIE). Most of these publications are available through the ERIC Document Reproduction Service (EDRS). For publications cited in this bibliography that are available from EDRS, ordering number and price code are included. Readers who wish to order a publication should write to the ERIC Document Reproduction Service, 7420 Fullerton Rd., Suite 110, Springfield, VA 22153-2852. (Phone orders with VISA or MasterCard are taken at 800-443-ERIC or 703-440-1400.) When ordering, please specify the document (ED) number. Documents are available as noted in microfiche (MF) and paper copy (PC). If you have the price code ready when you call EDRS, an exact price can be quoted. The last page of the latest issue of *Resources in Education* also has the current cost, listed by code.

Allen, Walter R. 1988. "Black Students in U.S. Higher Education: Toward Improved Access, Adjustment, and Achievement." *Urban Review* 20(3): 165–88.

Alvarez, Anna Isabel, et al. 1984. *Black and Latino Transfer Barriers at City College of San Francisco: A Pilot Study.* San Francisco: City College of San Francisco. ED 243 541. 64 pp. MF–01; PC–03.

American Council on Education. 1989. *1989–90 Fact Book on Higher Education.* New York: ACE/Macmillan.

American Council on Education and Business–Higher Education Forum. 1990. *Three Realities.* Washington, D.C.: Author.

American Council on Education and Education Commission of the States. 1988. *One-Third of a Nation.* A report of the Commission on Minority Participation in Education and American Life. Washington, D.C.: Author.

Arvizu, S., and T. Arciniega. 1985. "What Colleges Must Do to Achieve Quality and Equity: A Campus-Based Case Study." Paper presented at the 45th ETS Invitational Conference, October 1984, New York, New York.

Ascher, Carol. July 1983. "Helping Minority Students with Nontraditional Skills Enter and Complete College." ED 234 104. 5 pp. MF–01; PC–01.

Astin, Alexander W. 1975. *Preventing Students from Dropping Out.* San Francisco: Jossey-Bass.

Astin, A.W., and K.P. Cross. 1979. *Student Financial Aid and Persistence in College.* Los Angeles: Univ. of California–Los Angeles, Higher Education Research Institute. ED 221 078. 412 pp. MF–01; PC–17.

Astin, A.W., B. Fuller, and K.C. Green. 1978. "Admitting and Assisting Students after *Bakke.*" New Directions for Higher Education No. 23. San Francisco: Jossey-Bass.

Astin, Alexander W., et al. 1982. *Minorities in American Higher Education.* San Francisco: Jossey-Bass.

Astone, Barbara, Elsa Nuñez-Wormack, and Ivan Smodlaka. 1989. "Intensive Academic Advisement: A Model for Retention." *College and University* 65(1): 31–43.

Atelsek, Frank J., and Irene L. Gomberg. 1978. *Special Programs for Female and Minority Graduate Students.* Higher Education Panel Report No. 41. Washington, D.C.: American Council on Education. ED 163 863. 54 pp. MF–01; PC–03.

Badwound, Elgin, and William G. Tierney. 1988. "Leadership and American Indian Values: The Tribal College Dilemma." *Journal of American Indian Education* 28(1): 9–13.

Bagasao, Paula Y. November/December 1989. "Student Voices: Breaking the Silence. The Asian and Pacific American Experience." *Change:* 28–37.

Beal, Philip E., and Lee Noel. 1979. "Target Groups for Retention Strategies by Type of Institution." In *What Works in Student Retention.* Iowa City: American College Testing Program.

Bender, Louis W., and C. Blanco. 1987. "Programs to Enhance Participation, Retention, and Success of Minority Students at Florida Community Colleges and Universities." ED 288 582. 69 pp. MF–01; PC–03.

Bennis, W. 1990. "Reflections on Leadership." Speech delivered at an annual conference of the American Council on Education, January 17–19, Washington, D.C.

Berger, Joseph. 7 August 1988a. "Success Strategies." *N.Y. Times.*
———. 8 September 1988b. "More Businesses and Schools Join to Attack Illiteracy in Workplace." *N.Y. Times.*

Bermingham, Jack, et al. 1986. "Multicultural Education for the Classroom." Paper presented at an annual meeting of the Association of Teacher Educators, February, Atlanta, Georgia.

Bowler, Rosemarie, Stephen Rauch, and Rolf Schwarzer. 1986. "Self-Esteem and Interracial Attitudes in Black High School Students: A Comparison with Five Other Ethnic Groups." *Urban Education* 21(1): 3–19.

Carnegie Foundation for the Advancement of Teaching. 1989. *Tribal Colleges: Shaping the Future of Native America.* Princeton, N.J.: Princeton Univ. Press.

Carter, Deborah J., and Reginald Wilson. 1989. *Minorities in Higher Education.* Eighth annual status report. Washington, D.C.: American Council on Education.

Castillo, Max. 1984. "Underrepresentation of Minorities Who Transfer to Baccalaureate Institutions." San Antonio, Tex.: San Antonio College. ED 265 999. 12 pp. MF–01; PC–01.

Christoffel, Pamela. 1986. "Minority Student Access and Retention: A Research and Development Update." New York: College Entrance Examination Board. ED 279 217. 10 pp. MF–01; PC–01.

Clark, Katherine W. 1987. "Using Multiethnic Literature in the Composition Classroom: Overcoming the Obstacles." Paper presented at an annual conference of the Society for the Study of Multiethnic Literature of the United States, April 24–30, Irvine, California.

Cohen, Arthur M. 1981. "Institutional Factors Affecting Student Participation in Community College Science Programs." Paper presented at an annual meeting of the American Educational Research Association to the Special Interest Group on Community/Junior College Research, April 13–17, Los Angeles, California.

———. 1987. "Facilitating Degree Achievement by Minorities: The Community College Environment." Paper prepared for "Some Access to Achievement: Strategies for Urban Institutions," November 15–17, Los Angeles, California.

———. 1990. "The Transfer Indicator." Paper prepared for the annual convention of the American Association of Community and Junior Colleges, April 24, Seattle, Washington.

Cole, Ernestine B. 1986. *Urban Community College Transfer Opportunity Program: Annual Report.* Miami: Miami Dade Community College. ED 279 377. 68 pp. MF–01; PC–03.

Cole, Johnnetta. 1990. "Guest Postscript: Expectations for Academia." *Progressions* 2(3).

Commission on California State Postsecondary Education. January 1983. "The Core Student Affirmative Action Program at the California State University." Report 83–85. Sacramento: Author. ED 230 090. 25 pp. MF–01; PC–01.

———. June 1985. "Commission Staff Comments and Recommendations on Equal Educational Opportunity Programs for the 1984–85 Budget." Sacramento: Author. ED 255 132. 77 pp. MF–01; PC–04.

Commission on Florida State Postsecondary Education. March 1984. "The Master Plan for Florida Postsecondary Education." Tallahassee: Author. ED 279 271. 68 pp. MC-01; PC–03.

Committee on Education and Labor. 1985. "Staff Report on Hispanic Access to Higher Education." Washington D.C.: Author. ED 266 716. 37 pp. MF–01; PC–02.

Cox, A. 1979. "Minority Admissions after *Bakke.*" In Bakke, Weber, *and Affirmative Action.* Working Papers from a Rockefeller Foundation Conference. New York: Rockefeller Foundation.

Crook, David B., and David E. Lavin. 1989. "The Community College Effect Revisited: The Long-Term Impact of Community College Entry on B.A. Attainment." Paper presented at an annual meeting of the American Educational Research Association, March, San Francisco, California. ED 306 977. 36 pp. MF–01; PC–02.

Dix, Linda S. 1987. *Minorities: Their Underrepresentation and Career Differentials in Science and Engineering.* Washington, D.C.: National Research Council. ED 285 751. 174 pp. MF–01; PC–07.

Donovan, Richard A., and Barbara Schaier-Peleg. 1988. "Making

Transfer Work." *Change* 20(1): 33–37.

Dunston, F.M., et al. 1983. "Review of the Literature: Black Student Retention in Higher Education Institutions." Washington, D.C.: U.S. Dept. of Education, Office for Civil Rights. ED 228 912. 23 pp. MF–01; PC–01.

Dupuis, Victor L., and Margery W. Walker. 1988. "The Circle of Learning at Kickapoo." *Journal of American Indian Education* 28(1): 27–32.

Economist. 6 January 1990a. "Business, Gone Fishing" 314(7636): 61–62.

———. 3 March 1990b. "Black Americans" 314(7644): 17–19.

Elvin, Rebecca S., and Gerald L. Wood. 1989. "AAU Research Institution Pilots Transfer Institute to Enhance Minority Educational Opportunities." ED 308 921. 30 pp. MF–01; PC–02.

Enarson, Harold L. 1984. "The Ethical Imperative of the College Presidency." *Educational Record* 65(2): 24–26.

Estrada, L.F. 1988. "Anticipating the Demographic Future." *Change* 20(3): 14–19.

Fantini, M.D. 1981. "Anticipatory Leadership and Resource Management in the Future." *Theory into Practice* 22(4): 14–218.

Farrell, Charles S. 1989. "Institutions Deny Setting Quotas for Asian-American Admissions." *Black Issues in Higher Education* 6(3): 10–11.

Fast, R. 1977. "Educational Leadership: Proactive or Reactive?" *Challenge in Educational Administration* 16(1,2): 34–42.

Fernandez, Ricardo. 1989. "Five Cities High School Dropout Study: Characteristics of Hispanic High School Students." Washington, D.C.: ASPIRA Association.

Fields, Cheryl. 1988. "The Hispanic Pipeline: Narrow, Leaking, and Needing Repair." *Change* 20(3): 22–27.

Fincher, Cameron. 1975. "The Access-Placement-Retention-Graduation of Minority Students in Higher Education." Atlanta: Univ. of Georgia, Institute of Higher Education. ED 114 011. 68 pp. MF–01; PC–03.

Fisher, James J., Martha W. Tach, and Karen J. Wheeler. 1988. "Leadership Behaviors of Effective College Presidents." Paper presented at an annual meeting of the American Educational Research Association, April 5–8, New Orleans, Louisiana. ED 301 075. 50 pp. MF–01; PC–02.

Fleming, Jacqueline. 1984. *Blacks in College.* San Francisco: Jossey-Bass.

Forni, Jane. 1989. "Hispanics and the Neylan Colleges: The Potential and the Challenge." In *Current Issues in Catholic Higher Education,* edited by Sr. Alice Gallin, OSU. Washington, D.C.: Association of Catholic Colleges and Universities.

Galligani, Dennis J. 1984. "Changing the Culture of the University." ED 244 530. 70 pp. MF–01; PC–03.

Gardner, D.P. 1987. "The American University in Transition." Speech delivered at the Commonwealth Club of California, October 30, San Francisco, California.

Glennin, Robert E., and D.M. Basley. 1985. "Reduction of Attrition through Intrusive Advising." *NASPA Journal* 22(3): 10–14.

Gosman, Erica J., Betty A. Dandridge, Michael J. Nettles, and Robert A. Thoeny. 1983. "Predicting Student Progression: The Influence of Race and Other Student and Institutional Characteristics on College Student Performance." *Research in Higher Education* 18(2): 209–36.

Grant, Carl A. 1983. "Multicultural Teacher Education: Renewing the Discussion. A Response to Martin Haberman." *Journal of Teacher Education* 34(2): 29–32.

Green, Kenneth C. 1982. *Government Support for Minority Participation in Higher Education.* AAHE-ERIC Higher Education Research Report No. 9. Washington, D.C.: American Association for Higher Education. ED 226 688. 65 pp. MF–01; PC–03.

Green, Madeleine F., ed. 1989. *Minorities on Campus.* Washington, D.C.: American Council on Education.

Guichard, Gus, and Rita Cepeda. 1986. "Plan for Improving the Enrollment, Retention, and Transfer of Minority Students." ED 276 469. 50 pp. MF–01; PC–02.

Gurin, P., and E.G. Epps. 1975. *Black Consciousness, Identity, and Achievement.* New York: John Wiley & Sons.

Halcon, John J. 1988. "Exemplary Programs for College-Bound Minority Students." Boulder, Colo.: Western Interstate Commission for Higher Education. ED 298 830. 47 pp. MF–01; PC–02.

Hamilton, C. 1979. "On Affirmative Action as Public Policy." In Bakke, Weber, *and Affirmative Action.* Working Papers from a Rockefeller Foundation Conference. New York: Rockefeller Foundation.

Hanford, G. 1982. "Barriers to Education Revisited." In *Equality Postponed: Continuing Barriers to Higher Education in the 1980s,* edited by S. Adolphus. New York: College Entrance Examination Board.

Hardesty, Sarah. 1990. "Bridging the Financial Gap to Higher Education." *Progressions* 2(3): 4–6.

Himmelfarb, Gertrude. 5 May 1988. "Stanford and Duke Undercut Classical Values." *N.Y. Times.*

Hoachlander, E. Gareth, and Cynthia L. Brown. 1989. "Asians in Higher Education: Conflicts over Admissions." *NEA Higher Education Journal* 5(2): 5–20.

Hodgkinson, Harold L. 1983. "Guess Who's Coming to College: Your Students in 1990." Washington, D.C.: National Institute of Independent Colleges and Universities. ED 234 882. 4 pp. MF–01; PC–01.

———. 1985. "Demographics and the Economy: Understanding a Changing Marketplace." *Admissions Strategist* 3: 1–6.

———, ed. 1986. *Higher Education: Diversity Is Our Middle Name.* Washington, D.C.: National Institute of Independent Colleges and Universities.

Hsia, Jayjia, and Marsha Hirano-Nakanishi. 1988. "Asian-Americans Fight the Myth of the Super Student." *Educational Record* 68(4): 94–97.

———. November/December 1989. "The Demographics of Diversity: Asian-Americans and Higher Education." *Change:* 20–27.

Illinois Community College Board. 1986. "Minority Student Participation: Illinois Public Community College System, Fiscal Years 1983 through 1986." Springfield: Author.

Ingersoll, J. Ronald. 1988. *The Enrollment Problem.* New York: Macmillan.

Jackson, Gregory A. 1988. "Financial Aid and Minority Access: Why Do We Know So Little?" *Change* 20(5): 48–49.

Jaschik, Scott. 8 April 1987. "Education Dept. Reports on Desegregation but Includes No Evaluation of State Efforts." *Chronicle of Higher Education:* 18.

Jordan, James R. 1981. "Improving Basic Skills in Birmingham." In *A Tale of Three Cities: Boston, Birmingham, Hartford.* New York: Ford Foundation.

Kelly, Kathleen. 1989. "An Enabling Education: A Catholic College Contribution." *Current Issues in Catholic Higher Education* 9(2): 16–20.

Kimmel, Howard, Nancy Martino, and Reginald Tomkins. 1988. "An Approach to Increasing the Representation of Minorities in Engineering and Science." *Engineering Education* 78(11): 186–89.

Kleinfeld, Judith, Joe Cooper, and Nathan Kyle. 1987. "Postsecondary Counselors: A Model for Increasing Native Americans' College Success." *Journal of American Indian Education* 28(1): 9–15.

Langer, Peter. 1987. "Student Retention at a Nonresidential University." Boston: Univ. of Massachusetts at Boston, Office of Institutional Research and Planning.

Lapchick, Richard E. 1989. "Future of the Black Student-Athlete." *Educational Record* 70(2): 32–35.

Lavin, David E. 1974. *Open Admissions at The City University of New York: A Description of Academic Outcomes after Two Years.* New York: City Univ. of New York, Office of Program and Policy Research. ED 137 446. 265 pp. MF–01; PC–11.

Lenning, Oscar T., Philip E. Beal, and Ken Sauer. 1980. *Retention and Attrition: Evidence for Action and Research.* ED 192 661. 134 pp. MF–01; PC–06.

Lincoln, E.C. 1979. "In the Wake of *Bakke.*" In Bakke, Weber, *and Affirmative Action.* Working Papers from a Rockefeller Foundation Conference. New York: Rockefeller Foundation.

Loo, Chalsa M., and Garry Rolison. 1986. "Alienation of Ethnic Minority Students at a Predominantly White University." *Journal of

Higher Education 57(1): 58–77.

Lynton, E.A. 1981. "Colleges, Universities, and Corporate Training." In *Business and Higher Education: Toward New Alliances.* New Directions for Experiential Learning No. 13. San Francisco: Jossey-Bass.

McDaniel, R., and J. McKee. 1971. *An Evaluation of Higher Education's Response to Black Students.* Bloomington: Indiana Univ.

McIntosh, B.J., et al. 1987. *Native American Academic, Financial, Social, Psychological, and Demographic Implications for Education: A Challenge to Community College Administrators, Faculty, and Support Service Personnel.* Mesa, Ariz.: Mesa Community College, Office of Research and Development.

Madrid, Arturo. 1988. "Missing People and Others." *Change* 20(3): 54–59.

Magner, Denise K. 29 November 1989. "Colleges Try New Ways to Insure Minority Students Make It to Graduation." *Chronicle of Higher Education* 36(13): A1.

———. 14 November 1990. "Amid the Diversity, Racial Isolation Remains at Berkeley." *Chronicle of Higher Education* 37(2).

Mallinckrodt, Brent, and William E. Sedlacek. 1987. "Student Retention and the Use of Campus Facilities by Race." *NASPA Journal* 24(3): 28–32.

Mancini-Billson, Janet, and Margaret Brooks-Terry. Summer 1987. "A Student Retention Model for Higher Education." *College and University* 4: 290–305.

Martinez-Perez, L. 1978. "Hispanic Students in Higher Education." Paper presented at the National Conference on the Education of Hispanics, August 20–23, Alexandria, Virginia.

Melendez, S., and R. Wilson. 1985. *Minorities in Higher Education.* Fourth annual status report. Washington, D.C.: American Council on Education. ED 275 215. 27 pp. MF–01; PC–02.

Mendoza, Jose. 1988. "Developing and Implementing a Data Base and Microcomputer Tracking System to Track and Serve Minority Students to Enhance Minority Recruitment and Retention." ED 301 292. 33 pp. MF–01; PC–02.

Middleton, Ernest, and Emanual Mason, eds. 1987. *Recruitment and Retention of Minority Students in Teacher Education.* Monograph No. 8. Proceedings of the National Invitational Conference of Teacher Education, March 29–April 1, Lexington, Kentucky. ED 301 535. 158 pp. MF–01; PC–07.

Mingle, James R. 1987. *Focus on Minorities: Trends in Higher Education Participation and Success.* Denver: Education Commission of the States. ED 287 404. 50 pp. MF–01; PC–02.

Monsivais, George I., and Mark Bustillos. July 1990. "Understanding Latino Poverty in the U.S." *The Tomas Rivera Center Policy Gram.*

Murphy, Peter James. 1984. "Preparing Administrators for the Twenty-First Century." *Higher Education* 13: 439–49.

Naisbitt, John, and Patricia Aburdene. 1989–90. "Megatrends 2000." *Best of Business Quarterly* 11(4): 52–60.

National Action Council for Minorities in Engineering, Inc. 1988. *Annual Report.* New York: Author.

National Center for Postsecondary Governance and Finance. 1989. *The Bottom Line on Removing Race/Ethnicity as a Factor in College Completion.* Report No. 3. College Park, Md.: Author.

National Coalition of Advocates for Students. 1988. *New Voices: Immigrant Students in U.S. Public Schools.* Boston: Author.

National Puerto Rican Coalition. 1989. "Leadership Development Programs." *Newsletter* 9(4): 2.

National Research Council. 1989. *Everybody Counts: A Report to the Nation on the Future of Mathematics Education.* Washington, D.C.: National Academy Press.

Navarro, S. 1985. "The Quality Education Movement." Paper presented at the 45th ETS Invitational Conference, October 1984, New York, New York.

New York Times. 7 September 1988a. "U.S. Hispanic Population Is Up 34% since 1980."

———. 22 September 1988b. "School and College Graduates Put at Record Number in U.S."

———. 15 November 1988c. "Fewer Degrees for Black Men in Maryland."

Nicholson, Carol, Anne Law, Lise Vogel, Virginia Cyrus, and Mary Pinney. 1989. "Balancing the Curriculum and the Campus Environment at Rider College with Respect to Race, Class, and Gender, 1988–1989." Project sponsored by Rider College and the New Jersey Department of Higher Education. Lawrenceville, N.J.: Rider College.

Nora, Amaury. 1987. "Determinants of Retention among Chicano College Students: A Structural Model." *Research in Higher Education* 26(1): 31–59.

Nora, Amaury, and Fran Horvath. 1989. "Financial Assistance: Minority Enrollments and Persistence." *Education and Urban Society* 21(3): 299–309.

Nuñez-Wormack, Elsa. 1989. "The National Agenda for Higher Education into the Twenty-First Century." Keynote address at the Statewide Conference on the Retention of Minority Students, January 10, Columbus, Ohio. ED 306 332. 23 pp. MF–01; PC–01.

Nuss, E.M. 1989–90. "Carnegie Releases New Report." *NASPA Forum* 10(4): 3.

Oakland, Thomas D., and Maria L. Ramos-Cancel. 1985. "Educational and Psychological Perspectives on Hispanic Children from Hispanic Journals: A View from Latin America." *Journal of Multilingual and Multicultural Development* 6(1): 67–80.

O'Brien, Eileen M. 1990. "The Demise of Native American Education." *Black Issues in Higher Education* 7(1): 15–22.

Olivas, Michael A., ed. 1986. *Latino College Students*. New York: Columbia Univ., Teachers College Press.

Olivas, M., and N. Alimba. 1979. *The Dilemma of Access: Minorities in Two-Year Colleges*. Washington, D.C.: Howard Univ. Press.

Olstad, Roger T., et al. 1983. "Multicultural Education for Preservice Teachers." *Integrated Education* 21 (1–6): 137–39.

Orfield, Gary. 1988. "Exclusion of the Majority: Shrinking College Access and Public Policy in Metropolitan Los Angeles." *Urban Review* 20(3): 147–63.

Orfield, Gary, and Faith Paul. 1988. "Declines in Minority Access: A Tale of Five Cities." *Educational Record* 68(4): 57–62.

Oxford Analytica. 1986. *America in Perspective: Major Trends in the United States through the 1990s*. Boston: Houghton Mifflin.

Pascarella, Ernest T. 1986. "A Program for Research and Policy Development on Student Persistence at the Institutional Level." *Journal of College Student Personnel* 27(2): 100–107.

Pascarella, E., and D. Chapman. 1983. "A Multi-Institutional Path Analytic Validation of Tinto's Model of College Withdrawal." *American Educational Research Journal* 20(1): 87–102.

Payan, Rose M., et al. 1984. "Access to College for Mexican-Americans in the Southwest: Replication after 10 Years." Princeton, N.J.: Educational Testing Service. ED 250 978. 40 pp. MF–01; PC–02.

Pelletier, S.G., and W. McNamera. 1985. "To Market? Two Views." *Educational Horizons* 63(2): 54–60.

Pemberton, Gayle. 1988. *On Teaching the Minority Student: Problems and Strategies*. Brunswick, Me.: Bowdoin College.

Peterson, M.W., et al. 1979. *Black Students on White Campuses: The Impacts of Increased Black Enrollments*. Ann Arbor: Univ. of Michigan, Institute for Survey Research.

Porter, Oscar F. 1989. *Undergraduate Completion and Persistence at Four-Year Colleges and Universities*. Washington, D.C.: National Institute of Independent Colleges and Universities. HE 023 534. 30 pp. MF–01; PC–02.

Pratt, L., and N. Felder. 1982. "An Analysis of Variables Which Discriminate between Persisting and Nonpersisting Students." Paper presented at an annual forum of the Southern Association of Institutional Research, October 28–29, Birmingham, Alabama. ED 225 494. 11 pp. MF–01; PC–01.

Preer, Jean L. 1981. *Minority Access to Higher Education*. Higher Education Research Report No. 1. Washington, D.C.: American Association for Higher Education. ED 207 474. 55 pp. MF–01; PC–03.

Pulliams, Preston. 1988. "An Urban Community College Attempts to Assure Student Achievement: Creative Minority Initiatives." Paper presented at the National AACJC Conference, April 25, Philadelphia, Pennsylvania.

Ramon, Gilberto. 1985. "Counseling Hispanic College-Bound High School Students." ED 268 188. 86 pp. MF–01; PC–04.

Rendón, Laura I., and Amaury Nora. 1988. *Salvaging Minority Transfer Students: Toward New Policies that Facilitate Baccalaureate Attainment.* Carnegie Corporation Quality Education for Minorities Project. Cambridge: Massachusetts Institute of Technology. ED 305 098. 39 pp. MF–01; PC–02.

Reynolds, William Bradford. 1988. "Discrimination against Asian-Americans in Higher Education: Evidence, Causes, and Cures." Washington, D.C.: U.S. Dept. of Justice, Civil Rights Div. ED 308 730. 19 pp. MF–01; PC–01.

Richardson, Richard C. 1988. "Solving the Access/Quality Puzzle in Two-Year Colleges." Keynote address at the Ohio Conference on Access and Success, October 19, Columbus, Ohio. ED 300 096. 12 pp. MF–01; PC–01.

Richardson, R.C., Jr., and L.W. Bender. 1987. *Fostering Minority Access and Achievement.* San Francisco: Jossey-Bass.

Rivera, Manuel G. 1986. "Recruitment of Hispanic and Black Students." ED 280 670. 29 pp. MF–01; PC–02.

Robey, Bryant. 1985. *The American People.* New York: E.P. Dutton.

Rodriguez, Carmelo. 1982. "Selected Topics on Hispanic Access to Higher Education." Testimony before the National Commission on Excellence in Education, June 23, Chicago, Illinois. ED 237 023. 51 pp. MF–01; PC–03.

Rodriguez, Max. 1988. "Annual Report of the Urban Community College Transfer Opportunities Program." New York: City Univ. of New York, LaGuardia Community College.

Ross, Kathleen. 1986. "Making Diversity into a Practical Reality." In *Higher Education: Diversity Is Our Middle Name,* edited by Harold L. Hodgkinson. Washington, D.C.: National Institute of Independent Colleges and Universities.

Rossmann, E. Jack, Helen S. Astin, Alexander W. Astin, and Elaine H. El-Khawas. 1975. *Open Admission at City University of New York.* Englewood Cliffs, N.J.: Prentice-Hall.

Ryan, Charlotte. 1986. "From Community College to Glassboro State College: PROMIST--A Program for Minority Student Transfers." Glassboro, N.J.: Glassboro State College.

St. John, Edward P., and Jay Noell. 1989. "The Effects of Student Financial Aid on Access to Higher Education: An Analysis of Progress with Special Consideration of Minority Enrollment." *Research in Higher Education* 30(6): 563–81.

Samuels, Frank. 1985. "Closing the Door: The Future of Minorities in Two-Year Institutions." Paper presented at the National Adult Education Conference of the American Association for Adult and Continuing Education, November 7, Milwaukee, Wisconsin. ED 263 946. 31 pp. MF–01; PC–02.

Sanders, N.F. 1987. "What Minority Students Expect When They Transfer to Four-Year Colleges." *Admissions Strategist* 10: 35–41.

Sedlacek, William E., and Dennis W. Webster. 1977. "Admission and

Retention of Minority Students in Large Universities." *Journal of College Student Personnel* 19(3): 242–48.

Smith, Donald H. 1980. "Admissions and Retention Problems of Black Students at Seven Predominantly White Universities." ED 186 572. 42 pp. MF–01; PC–02.

South Carolina Commission on Higher Education. 1987. "Annual Report." Columbia: Author.

Spratten, Thaddeus. 1979. "The *Bakke* Decision: Implications for Black Educational and Professional Opportunities." *Journal of Negro Education* 48(4): 449–56.

Suen, H.K. March 1983. "Alienation and Attrition of Black College Students on a Predominantly White Campus." *Journal of College Student Personnel* 24: 117–21.

Suzuki, Bob H. November/December 1989. "Asian-Americans as the 'Model Minority': Outdoing Whites? or Media Hype?" *Change:* 12–19.

Taddiken, Nancy K. 1981. "Minorities on Campus: A Survey of Black and Hispanic Participation in Colleges of the Rochester Area." Rochester, N.Y.: Urban League, Inc.

Task Force on Women, Minorities, and the Handicapped in Science and Technology. 1988. "Changing America: The New Face of Science and Engineering." Washington, D.C.: Author.

Taylor, K. 1983. "A Coast-to-Coast Sampling of Innovative Hispanic Programs." *CASE Currents.* Washington, D.C.: Council for Advancement and Support of Education.

Teisman, P.M. 1985. "Study of Mathematics Performance of Blacks at the University of California–Berkeley." Doctoral dissertation, Univ. of California–Berkeley.

Tinto, Vincent. Winter 1975. "Dropout from Higher Education: A Theoretical Synthesis of Recent Research." *Review of Educational Research* 45: 89–125.

———. 1987. *Leaving College: Rethinking the Causes and Cures of Student Attrition.* Chicago: Univ. of Chicago Press.

———. 1989. "The Principles of Effective Retention." Speech presented at an annual meeting of the Association for Institutional Research, April 30, Baltimore, Maryland.

Tokuyama, M. Yukie. 1989. "New Demographics Reveal the 'Invisible' Asians." *Educational Record* 70(2): 68–69.

Trevino, C., and B. Wise. 1980. "Summer Acceptance Program: A Viable Option for Provisional Students Entering a Private University." Paper presented at an annual meeting of the Western Reading Association, March 27–30, San Francisco, California. ED 188 118. 9 pp. MF–01; PC–01.

Turner, Rick. 1980. "Factors Influencing the Retention of Minority Students in the 1980s: Opinions and Impressions." *Journal of Non-White Concerns* 8(4): 204–15.

Tysinger, James W., and Mary F. Whiteside. 1987. "A Review of Recruitment and Retention Programs for Minority and Disadvantaged Students in Health Professions Education." *Journal of Allied Health* 16(3): 209–17.

U.S. Bureau of the Census. 1980a. "Nosotros...We...." Washington, D.C.: Government Printing Office.

———. 1980b. "We, the Asian and Pacific Islander Americans." Washington, D.C.: Government Printing Office.

———. 1980c. "We, the First Americans." Washington, D.C.: Government Printing Office.

———. May 1983. "General Population Characteristics—1980." U.S. Summary Series PC 80-1-Bl. Washington, D.C.: Government Printing Office.

———. July 1989. "Hispanic Population in the U.S.—March 1988." Supplement to *Current Population Reports*. Population Characteristics, Series P-20, No. 438. Washington, D.C.: Government Printing Office.

———. March 1990a. "Current Population Survey." Unpublished data. Washington, D.C.: U.S. Dept. of Commerce.

———. May 1990b. "Hispanic Population in the U.S.—March 1989." *Current Population Reports*. Population Characteristics, Series P-20, No. 444. Washington, D.C.: Government Printing Office.

———. September 1990c. "Money, Income, and Poverty Status in the United States—1989." *Current Population Reports,* Series P-60, No. 168. Washington, D.C.: Government Printing Office.

U.S. Congress, House of Representatives. November 1985. "Staff Report on Hispanic Access to Higher Education of the Committee on Education and Labor." Washington, D.C.: Government Printing Office. ED 266 716. 37 pp. MF–01; PC–02.

U.S. Dept. of Education, National Center for Education Statistics. 1984. "Higher Education General Information Survey, Fall Enrollment and Compliance Report of Institutions of Higher Education, 1984." Washington, D.C.: Author.

———. February 1989, updated 1990. "Fall Enrollment in Colleges and Universities" and "Integrated Postsecondary Education Data System Fall Enrollment, 1986." Washington, D.C.: Author.

U.S. Dept. of Labor, Bureau of Labor Statistics. January 1990a. "Employment and Earnings." *Current Population Survey.* Washington, D.C.: Government Printing Office.

———. April 1990b. "Outlook 2000." Bureau Bulletin No. 2352, table A1. Washington, D.C.: Government Printing Office.

Van Alstyne, Arvo. 1978. "From Discrimination to Affirmative Action." ED 202 379. 12 pp. MF–01; PC–01.

Velez, William, and Rajshekhar G. Javalgi. November 1987. "Two-Year College to Four-Year College: The Likelihood of Transfer." *American Journal of Education* 62: 81–94.

Wang, L. Ling-Chi. 1988. "Meritocracy and Diversity in Higher Education: Discrimination against Asian-Americans in the Post-*Bakke*

Era." *Urban Review* 20(3): 189–209.

Warfield, Deborah. 1985. "Florida Keys Community College's Reach-Out Program." ED 272 259. 24 pp. MF–01; PC–01.

West, Carolyn, John Simpson, and Charles W. Jones. 1975. "Minority Retention in a Community College Program for the Disadvantaged." ED 151 660. 23 pp. MF–01; PC–01.

Wilbur, Franklin P., et. al. 1988. "School-College Partnerships: A Look at the Major National Models." ED 291 320. 65 pp. MF–01; PC–03.

Wiley, Ed, III. 1989. "Native American Educational Plight Described as National Disgrace." *Black Issues in Higher Education* 6(3): 8–9.

Wilson, Reginald. 1986. "Minority Participation in Community Colleges." ED 271 159. 15 pp. MF–01; PC–01.

Woodland, Calvin E., and Marc S. Goldstein. 1984. "Facilitating Community College Access for Minority Students." ED 247 994. 14 pp. MF–01; PC–01.

Wright, Stephen J. 1978. "Testing/Admissions: What Can and Cannot Be Done." ED 202 380. 12 pp. MF–01; PC–01.

Zita, Jacquelyn. 1988. "Some Orthodoxy to Pluralism: A Postsecondary Curricular Reform." *Journal of Education* 170(2): 58–76.

INDEX

A

Academic support programs, 69
Academic transfer programs, 57
Admission practices, 49
Admissions
       contracts, 87
       minority recruitment, 41
       philosophies, 41
Affirmative action, 11
African-American community
       geographic distribution, 20
       median family income, 20
       population trends, 19
       socioeconomic status, 19
African-American men
       college drop out rate, 47
African-Americans
       in work force, 2
Afro-American studies, 42
Alternative admissions, 86
       criteria, 10, 50
American Association of Community and Junior Colleges, 56
American Indian community
       geographic distribution, 27
       population trends, 26
       socioeconomic status, 27
American Indian community colleges, 59
American Indian studies, 42
American Indians
       in labor force, 2
Arizona State University, 95
Arizona, University of, 61
Asian and Pacific Islander Communities, 24
       geographic distribution, 25-26
       population trends, 25
       socioeconomic status, 25
Asian studies, 42
Asians
       in labor force, 2
Athletics-related recruiting, 88

B

Bakke case, 11
Barry University (Florida)
       transfer policy, 57
Birthrates
       African-Americans, 16

E

Economic Opportunity Act of 1964, 7
"Educational pipeline", 1
Enrollment
        institutions of higher education, 3
Ethnic studies programs, 68, 78
Exploratory Transfer Institute, 61

F

Faculty-student contact, 92
Fifth Year Free program, 89
Financial aid, 50-53
Four plus One programs, 89

G

Geographic distribution
        minorities, 15
Glassboro State College, 60

H

High school graduates
        minorities, 4
High school teachers as recruiters, 96
Higher education
        racial integration, 7
Higher Education Amendments of 1968, 7
Higher Education Research Institute, 49
Hispanic community, 21
        geographic distribution, 24
        median family income, 23
        population trends, 22
        socioeconomic status, 23
Hispanics
        in labor force, 2
Hostos Community College, 94
Hunter College, 66

I

Immigration, 15, 45
Information centers
        urban areas, 93
Institutional audit, 48
Institutional commitment
        college presidents, 39
        financial support, 39
        minority recruitment, 39
        moral support, 42

to cultural diversity, 39

J

Joint admissions programs, 87

L

Labor force projections, 2
La Guardia Community College, 47, 87
Links to minority communities, 43

M

Maryland, University of, 12
Massachusetts, University of, 87
Median family income, 16
MESA (Mathematics, Engineering Science Achievement) program, 47
Mesa Community College (Arizona), 58
Miami University of
        transfer policy, 59
Minorities
        academic preparation, 49
        college drop out rate, 1
        economic condition, 2
        educational condition, 2
        exclusion from higher education, 47
        high school drop out rate, 1, 4
        recruitment and transfer, 56–61
        retention in college, 48, 53–55
        social condition, 2
        undereducation, 3
Minority affairs offices, 41
Minority faculty
        role models, 93
Minority recruitment
        administrators, 81
        counselors and professional staff, 84–85
        implementation, 85
        institutional research, 75
        models of organization, 85
        strategies, 71
        plan design, 71
Minority students
        academic profile, 75
        enrollment by curriculum, 77
        enrollments, 75–76
        graduation rates, 76
        retention rates, 76
        social integration, 78

Recruitment
>by high school counselors, 96
>institutional attitudes, 40
>minority faculty involvement, 42
>minority students, 3, 10, 12, 39, 40
>plan evaluation, 79–81
>team members, 42

Restricted enrollments, 14
"Revolving door", 48
Rider College, 64
Rochester, University of, 53, 89
Role models
>administrators, 68
>faculty, 67

S

Scholarships and financial aid, 88
Scholastic Aptitude Test, 50
Science and Technology Entry Program, 90
Science and Technology students, 13
Social activities
>recruitment through, 96–97
Social programs, 69
South Dakota, University of
>collaboration with tribal colleges, 60
Southern California, University of, 47
Strategies for counselors, 93
"Student ambassadors", 96
Student/institution fit model, 48

T

Texas, University of
>SHARE program, 94
"Transfer college", 61
Transfer policy
>California, 59
>Florida, 58
>Michigan, 59
>New Jersey, 59
Transfer programs, 87
Transfer students
>financial aid, 58
>from community colleges, 57
>interinstitutional collaboration, 59

U

United Negro College Fund, 61

V

Vassar
      joint admissions program, 60
Virginia State University, 8
Valencia Community College, 96

W

Wesleyan College, 94

ASHE-ERIC HIGHER EDUCATION REPORTS

Since 1983, the Association for the Study of Higher Education (ASHE) and the Educational Resources Information Center (ERIC) Clearinghouse on Higher Education, a sponsored project of the School of Education and Human Development at The George Washington University, have cosponsored the *ASHE-ERIC Higher Education Report* series. The 1990 series is the nineteenth overall and the second to be published by the School of Education and Human Development at the George Washington University.

Each monograph is the definitive analysis of a tough higher education problem, based on thorough research of pertinent literature and insitutional experiences. Topics are identified by a national survey. Noted practitioners and scholars are then commissioned to write the reports, with experts providing critical reviews of each manuscript before publication.

Eight monographs (10 before 1985) in the ASHE-ERIC Higher Education Report series are published each year and are available on individual and subscription basis. Subscription to eight issues is $80.00 annually; $60 to members of AAHE, AIR, or AERA; and $50 to ASHE members. All foreign subscribers must include an additional $10 per series year for postage.

To order single copies of existing reports, use the order form on the last page of this book. Regular prices, and special rates available to members of AAHE, AIR, AERA and ASHE, are as follows:

Series	Regular	Members
1990	$17.00	$12.75
1988-89	15.00	11.25
1985-87	10.00	7.50
1983-84	7.50	6.00
before 1983	6.50	5.00

Price includes book rate postage within the U.S. For foreign orders, please add $1.00 per book. Fast United Parcel Service available within the contiguous U.S. at $2.50 for each order under $50.00, and calculated at 5% of invoice total for orders $50.00 or above.

All orders under $45.00 must be prepaid. Make check payable to ASHE-ERIC. For Visa or MasterCard, include card number, expiration date and signature. A bulk discount of 10% is available on orders of 15 or more books (not applicable on subscriptions).

Address order to
ASHE-ERIC Higher Education Reports
The George Washington University
1 Dupont Circle, Suite 630
Washington, DC 20036
Or phone (202) 296-2597
Write or call for a complete catalog of ASHE-ERIC Higher Education Reports.

1990 ASHE-ERIC Higher Education Reports

1. The Campus Green: Fund Raising in Higher Education
   Barbara E. Brittingham and Thomas R. Pezzullo

2. The Emeritus Professor: Old Rank - New Meaning
   James E. Mauch, Jack W. Birch, and Jack Matthews

3. "High Risk" Students in Higher Education: Future Trends
   Dionne J. Jones and Betty Collier Watson

4. Budgeting for Higher Education at the State Level: Enigma,
   Paradox, and Ritual
   Daniel T. Layzell and Jan W. Lyddon

5. Proprietary Schools: Programs, Policies, and Prospects
   John B. Lee and Jamie P. Merisotis

6. College Choice: Understanding Student Enrollment Behavior
   Michael B. Paulsen

1989 ASHE-ERIC Higher Education Reports

1. Making Sense of Administrative Leadership: The 'L' Word in
   Higher Education
   Estela M. Bensimon, Anna Neumann, and Robert Birnbaum

2. Affirmative Rhetoric, Negative Action: African-American and
   Hispanic Faculty at Predominantly White Universities
   Valora Washington and William Harvey

3. Postsecondary Developmental Programs: A Traditional Agenda
   with New Imperatives
   Louise M. Tomlinson

4. The Old College Try: Balancing Athletics and Academics in
   Higher Education
   John R. Thelin and Lawrence L. Wiseman

5. The Challenge of Diversity: Involvement or Alienation in the
   Academy?
   Daryl G. Smith

6. Student Goals for College and Courses: A Missing Link in Assessing and Improving Academic Achievement
   Joan S. Stark, Kathleen M. Shaw, and Malcolm A. Lowther

7. The Student as Commuter: Developing a Comprehensive Institutional Response
   Barbara Jacoby

8. Renewing Civic Capacity: Preparing College Students for Service
   and Citizenship
   Suzanne W. Morse

1988 ASHE-ERIC Higher Education Reports

1. The Invisible Tapestry: Culture in American Colleges and Universities
   George D. Kuh and Elizabeth J. Whitt

2. Critical Thinking: Theory, Research, Practice, and Possibilities
   Joanne Gainen Kurfiss

3. Developing Academic Programs: The Climate for Innovation
   Daniel T. Seymour

4. Peer Teaching: To Teach is To Learn Twice
   Neal A. Whitman

5. Higher Education and State Governments: Renewed Partnership, Cooperation, or Competition?
   Edward R. Hines

6. Entrepreneurship and Higher Education: Lessons for Colleges, Universities, and Industry
   James S. Fairweather

7. Planning for Microcomputers in Higher Education: Strategies for the Next Generation
   Reynolds Ferrante, John Hayman, Mary Susan Carlson, and Harry Phillips

8. The Challenge for Research in Higher Education: Harmonizing Excellence and Utility
   Alan W. Lindsay and Ruth T. Neumann

1987 ASHE-ERIC Higher Education Reports

1. Incentive Early Retirement Programs for Faculty: Innovative Responses to a Changing Environment
   Jay L. Chronister and Thomas R. Kepple, Jr.

2. Working Effectively with Trustees: Building Cooperative Campus Leadership
   Barbara E. Taylor

3. Formal Recognition of Employer-Sponsored Instruction: Conflict and Collegiality in Postsecondary Education
   Nancy S. Nash and Elizabeth M. Hawthorne

4. Learning Styles: Implications for Improving Educational Practices
   Charles S. Claxton and Patricia H. Murrell

5. Higher Education Leadership: Enhancing Skills through Professional Development Programs
   Sharon A. McDade

6. Higher Education and the Public Trust: Improving Stature in Colleges and Universities
   Richard L. Alfred and Julie Weissman

7. College Student Outcomes Assessment: A Talent Development Perspective
Maryann Jacobi, Alexander Astin, and Frank Ayala, Jr.

8. Opportunity from Strength: Strategic Planning Clarified with Case Examples
Robert G. Cope

1986 ASHE-ERIC Higher Education Reports

1. Post-tenure Faculty Evaluation: Threat or Opportunity?
Christine M. Licata

2. Blue Ribbon Commissions and Higher Education: Changing Academe from the Outside
Janet R. Johnson and Laurence R. Marcus

3. Responsive Professional Education: Balancing Outcomes and Opportunities
Joan S. Stark, Malcolm A. Lowther, and Bonnie M.K. Hagerty

4. Increasing Students' Learning: A Faculty Guide to Reducing Stress among Students
Neal A. Whitman, David C. Spendlove, and Claire H. Clark

5. Student Financial Aid and Women: Equity Dilemma?
Mary Moran

6. The Master's Degree: Tradition, Diversity, Innovation
Judith S. Glazer

7. The College, the Constitution, and the Consumer Student: Implications for Policy and Practice
Robert M. Hendrickson and Annette Gibbs

8. Selecting College and University Personnel: The Quest and the Question
Richard A. Kaplowitz

1985 ASHE-ERIC Higher Education Reports

1. Flexibility in Academic Staffing: Effective Policies and Practices
Kenneth P. Mortimer, Marque Bagshaw, and Andrew T. Masland

2. Associations in Action: The Washington, D.C. Higher Education Community
Harland G. Bloland

3. And on the Seventh Day: Faculty Consulting and Supplemental Income
Carol M. Boyer and Darrell R. Lewis

4. Faculty Research Performance: Lessons from the Sciences and Social Sciences
John W. Creswell

5. Academic Program Review: Institutional Approaches, Expectations, and Controversies
   Clifton F. Conrad and Richard F. Wilson

6. Students in Urban Settings: Achieving the Baccalaureate Degree
   Richard C. Richardson, Jr. and Louis W. Bender

7. Serving More Than Students: A Critical Need for College Student Personnel Services
   Peter H. Garland

8. Faculty Participation in Decision Making: Necessity or Luxury?
   Carol E. Floyd

1984 ASHE-ERIC Higher Education Reports

1. Adult Learning: State Policies and Institutional Practices
   K. Patricia Cross and Anne-Marie McCartan

2. Student Stress: Effects and Solutions
   Neal A. Whitman, David C. Spendlove, and Claire H. Clark

3. Part-time Faulty: Higher Education at a Crossroads
   Judith M. Gappa

4. Sex Discrimination Law in Higher Education: The Lessons of the Past Decade. ED 252 169.*
   J. Ralph Lindgren, Patti T. Ota, Perry A. Zirkel, and Nan Van Gieson

5. Faculty Freedoms and Institutional Accountability: Interactions and Conflicts
   Steven G. Olswang and Barbara A. Lee

6. The High Technology Connection: Academic/Industrial Cooperation for Economic Growth
   Lynn G. Johnson

7. Employee Educational Programs: Implications for Industry and Higher Education. ED 258 501.*
   Suzanne W. Morse

8. Academic Libraries: The Changing Knowledge Centers of Colleges and Universities
   Barbara B. Moran

9. Futures Research and the Strategic Planning Process: Implications for Higher Education
   James L. Morrison, William L. Renfro, and Wayne I. Boucher

10. Faculty Workload: Research, Theory, and Interpretation
    Harold E. Yuker

1983 ASHE-ERIC Higher Education Reports

1. The Path to Excellence: Quality Assurance in Higher Education
   Laurence R. Marcus, Anita O. Leone, and Edward D. Goldberg

2. Faculty Recruitment, Retention, and Fair Employment: Obligations and Opportunities
   John S. Waggaman

3. Meeting the Challenges: Developing Faculty Careers. ED 232 516.*
   Michael C.T. Brooks and Katherine L. German

4. Raising Academic Standards: A Guide to Learning Improvement
   Ruth Talbott Keimig

5. Serving Learners at a Distance: A Guide to Program Practices
   Charles E. Feasley

6. Competence, Admissions, and Articulation: Returning to the Basics in Higher Education
   Jean L. Preer

7. Public Service in Higher Education: Practices and Priorities
   Patricia H. Crosson

8. Academic Employment and Retrenchment: Judicial Review and Administrative Action
   Robert M. Hendrickson and Barbara A. Lee

9. Burnout: The New Academic Disease. ED 242 255.*
   Winifred Albizu Meléndez and Rafael M. de Guzmán

10. Academic Workplace: New Demands, Heightened Tensions
    Ann E. Austin and Zelda F. Gamson

*Out-of-print. Available through EDRS. Call 1-800-443-ERIC.